THE MASTERS

1934 · 1935 · 1936 · 1937 · 1938 · 1939 · 1940 · 1941 · 1942 · 1946 · 1947 · 1948

THE MASTERS

The Story of Golf's Greatest Tournament

BY TOM FLAHERTY

HOLT, RINEHART AND WINSTON • NEW YORK

1949 · 1950 · 1951 · 1952 · 1953 · 1954 · 1955 · 1956 · 1957 · 1958 · 1959 · 1960

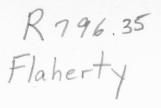
Published simultaneously in Canada by Holt, Rinehart
and Winston of Canada, Limited.

First Edition

The quotation from *Time* magazine in the chapter covering the 1946 Masters
is reprinted here through the courtesy of Time; copyright Time, Inc., 1946.

Library of Congress Catalog Card Number: 61-7631

82851-0111
Designer: Ernst Reichl
Printed in the United States of America

For Sally

INTRODUCTION

The Masters tournament began in 1934 at about the same time that I was trying out my first set of cut-down golf clubs as a kid in Latrobe, Pennsylvania. Even in those early years the Masters meant something special to anyone who was interested in golf. Part of it was the presence of Bob Jones—this was the one time each year that Bob would come out of retirement and try to win one more big one. Partly it was the Augusta National course itself, which everyone knew Bob had helped to design. And partly it was the way the players were selected, by personal invitation to those men who had earned the right to be there. No matter how you fare in the Masters it always feels good to be invited.

I had my first chance to play in the Masters in 1955, and that's when I began to understand why the Masters means so much to so many people. Jones was still very much there, not playing, unfortunately, but following the play closely from his cart. Somehow a wave and a word from Bob can make any golfer feel that all is right with the world. The beauty and the challenge of the course, along with the caliber of the competition, make a man feel that he must rise to his best performance, both personally and professionally.

This same attitude has an effect on the spectators, too. The gallery at Augusta is the best informed, best marshaled, and best mannered in America. And that becomes more important all the time, because the attendance at last year's tournament was more than 100,000 and at the end of the last day it seemed as if all of that number were trying to jam around the 18th green.

One reason for the intelligent spectator performance is that most of them are golfers themselves. When you see the collection of license plates from every state in the big parking lot and the long lines of private planes at the Augusta airports you realize that the most dedicated golf buffs in the country are in town. Then, too, the Masters has originated several features that make life more pleasant for both the player and the spectator. Multiple scoreboards, located at a dozen key places around the course, are kept up to the minute by a crew of 125 using a permanent underground telephone system. On several holes the fairways are completely roped off, so that everyone can see the play better and we players don't get caught in traffic jams. At 16 different places spectators can watch from mounds and terraces, which have been developed especially as vantage points for them. Even the uniformed gallery guards and marshals, the good refreshment and comfort facilities, and the free parking add something to the atmosphere of the Masters.

I think what it comes down to is that the customer is not treated as a necessary nuisance but as an important and welcome part of the tournament. The player gets that same feeling. Every time my wife and I turn off the main highway and drive through the tunnel of magnolias that leads to the old clubhouse it's like moving from one world into another —a special world made up of the things that are best in golf. I hope we'll be making that trip down Magnolia Lane for a long time to come.

—Arnold Palmer

ACKNOWLEDGMENTS The author expresses his gratitude to the editors of *Sports Illustrated* for permission to use the four-color plates, which capture so well the beauty of the Augusta National course. I am also grateful to Robert Jones, Clifford Roberts, and Mrs. Helen Harris of the Masters staff, for their parts in making this book possible; and to William MacPhail, Jimmy Dolan, and the CBS sports staff for their assistance at the 1960 Masters. A special word of thanks goes to Miss Toby Grayson, who assisted with the research; to Joe Fox, James Ellison, Sidney Satenstein, and Louise Waller; and to many other individuals not here named, who contributed information and encouragement to the final product.

—T.F.

THE MASTERS

THE BEGINNING

SURROUNDED by a bodyguard of United States Marines a happy young man in knickers moved slowly through the human storm around him toward the clubhouse at Merion. He did his best to acknowledge the accolades that this jubilant mob of 15,000 were offering him. It was September, 1930, and Robert Tyre Jones, Jr., had just won the U.S. Amateur championship, the last leg of the Grand Slam. By winning the British Amateur, the British Open, the U.S. Open, and now the U.S. Amateur in a single year he had accomplished the "impregnable quadrilateral." No man had done it before, and it seemed unlikely that any man could ever do it again. It was the supreme accomplishment of an already exceptional career.

But at twenty-eight Bob Jones was tired. He had no more golf worlds to conquer. The game which once had brought him so much satisfaction now was a joyless thing for him. Each new victory brought increased demands for still another victory. For fourteen years, just half of his lifetime, Jones had been fighting the battle of tournament golf. He was tired of the pyschological strain each victory represented. Tired, too, of living in the public eye like a matinee idol. For years Bob Jones had thought of quitting. If possible he wanted to quit on a high note. If that opportunity did not present itself then he would just slip quietly away. This moment, he knew, was the time he had been waiting for. To the dismay of millions of fans in a dozen lands Bob Jones turned away from tournament golf.

Jones set about rearranging his life with the same concentration he had applied to winning tournaments. He at last was able to devote some time to his law practice and business interests at home in Atlanta, Georgia. He played golf, but on his own terms: weekend foursomes with his old friends at the East Lake Club, where he had learned the game. For the first time he accepted the lucrative commercial offers he had been turning down for years in order to retain his amateur standing. He agreed to design Jones-model clubs for Spalding. He went on the air with a weekly half-hour radio broadcast in partnership with his friend and biographer, O.B. Keeler. He signed a contract with Warner Brothers and made two series of short, instructional movies. They were among the best and most successful movies of their kind ever produced.

At the same time Jones let it be known that he was ready to carry out another plan that had been forming in his mind for years. This plan was to design and build a golf course. After playing on the finest courses in the world for fourteen years Bob had some definite ideas on what a golf course should, and should not, be like. Jones's course would incorporate his ideas, and in a way be his contribution to the game. It would also be a retreat, where Bob and his friends from around the country could enjoy the game they loved in beautiful surroundings and with a degree of blessed privacy.

Promoters and others were quick to propose to Bob a number of sites and schemes for building the new course. They knew that any promotion Jones signed his name to was sure of success. Two basic requirements limited the choice of sites. It must be in the South, where Robert T. Jones was the most popular hero since Robert E. Lee; and it should be in Georgia, Bob's home state, within reasonable distance of Atlanta.

Among those who knew of and understood Jones's desire to build a course was Clifford Roberts of New York. Roberts, tall, bespectacled week-end golfer and successful Wall Street investment banker, had been introduced to Jones by mutual friends at a tournament a few years earlier. Roberts was an occasional vacationer in Augusta, Georgia, which happened also to be the home of Jones's wife and the site of the Southeastern Open, which Bob had regularly played in and won.

Roberts knew Jones wanted to stay clear of real-estate promotions, and he also knew of a particular piece of property a few miles west of Augusta which was for sale at depression prices. He invited Jones to come over and see it. Jones agreed, and on a December morning in 1930, in company with Cliff Roberts and Alfred Bourne, a member of the Singer Sewing Machine family, who had a winter home in Augusta, Bob had his first look at the land that was to become the Augusta National course.

In 1857, four years before the Civil War, a Belgian nobleman and horticulturist named Baron Prosper Jules Alphonse Berckmans had bought up an old indigo plantation near Augusta named "Fruitlands." Berckmans turned the property into the first nursery in the South. He planted magnolia seeds along the borders of the drive that led to his manor house. Near the house he planted Spanish cork oak, Chinese fir, and holly and an ornamental hedge. Among the stately pine forests on his 365 acres Berckmans indulged his horticulture hobby to its full extent. Azaleas flourished in abundance, in harmony with camellia bushes, yellow jasmine, woodbine, redbud, and dogwood.

Jones has recorded what he felt, as he turned off the highway and rode down the long archway of magnolia trees to the manor house.

"I stood at the top of the hill before that fine old house," said Jones, "and looked at the wide stretch of land rolling down the slope before me. It was cleared land, for the most part, and you could take in the vista all the way down to Rae's Creek. I knew instantly it was the kind of terrain I had always hoped to find. I had been told, of course, about the marvelous trees and plants, but I was still unprepared for the great bonus of beauty Fruitlands offered. Frankly, I was overwhelmed by the exciting possibilities of a golf course set in the midst of such a nursery."

With the site chosen, Roberts and Jones set to work organizing. They approached a number of their friends around the country. These were men of means, mostly, men who shared a common dedication: a love of good golf and golfing companionship. A holding company was formed with Fielding Wallace, an Augusta textile manufacturer, as a key member to buy the land. Plans for a private club were mapped out, with Jones as president and membership selected on a national basis (a maximum of thirty members to come from Augusta itself). Initiation fee was put at $350 with annual dues of $60. The only assessments would be voluntary.

Alister MacKenzie, a famed Scottish golf architect, agreed to collaborate with Jones in laying out the course, and in the spring of 1931 their work began.

Jones's intention was to construct an original course that would take advantage of the natural beauty and built-in hazards that Fruitlands offered. He wanted the course to rise out of the terrain, not to be stamped upon it. Jones was opposed to the rule of golf course design which prevailed then. This was the "penal" system in which the player is instantly penalized, usually by a man-made hazard, whenever he strays from the straight and narrow path. Instead, Jones was a disciple of the "strategic" design, in which each hole offers the player several alternate lines of attack. This permits the player, as he judges his own capacities and how the hole is playing that day, to choose either conservative, mildly aggressive, or audacious tactics. He is rewarded in proper proportion to the type of shot attempted and how well it was played.

6

Courses built to the "penal" standard often had upwards of two hundred bunkers. The design for the Augusta National called for twenty-two.

Architect MacKenzie offered these essentials for an "ideal" course:

1. A really great course must be pleasurable to the greatest number possible.

2. It must require strategy as well as skill, otherwise it cannot be enduringly interesting.

3. It must give the average player a fair chance, and at the same time require the utmost from the expert who tries for sub-par scores.

4. All natural beauty should be preserved, natural hazards should be utilized, and a minimum of artificiality introduced.

Writing years later in *Sports Illustrated*, Jones outlined his "strategic" approach to the design of the course:

Our overall aim at the Augusta National was to provide a golf course of considerable natural beauty, enjoyable for the average golfer and at the same time testing for the expert player striving to better par. We want to make the bogeys easy, if frankly sought, pars readily obtainable by standard good play, and birdies, except on par fives, dearly bought. Obviously with a course as wide open as is needed to accommodate the average golfer, we can only tighten it up by increasing the difficulty of play around the hole. This we attempt to do . . . by placing the flags in more difficult and exacting positions and by increasing the speed of the greens. Additionally, we try to maintain our greens at such firmness that they will not hold a misplayed shot. Generally speaking, the greens at Augusta are quite large and rolling, with carefully contrived undulations, the effect of which is magnified as the speed of the surfaces is increased.

Jones also disdained extremely long par 5 holes on which "you don't start playing golf until your third shot." He designed his par fives so the green can be reached with two excellent shots, which put the player in position to putt for an eagle or a birdie. But he also used hazards, notably the creek in front of the 13th and 15th greens, which penalize

7

the player who overestimates himself, tries for the green, and fails. On Jones's par fives the player is required to think. He must analyze his position, judge how badly he needs a birdie, and finally decide whether to accept the temptation or to play safely short of the hazard for his par.

By autumn of 1932 the course was ready. Each of the eighteen holes was named for the flowering plant that flourished along its borders. A small but handsome clubhouse had been built in old Southern plantation style, with the original Berckmans manor house as its heart. Ed Dudley, Jones's personal choice, was hired as resident professional. Some hundred charter members enjoyed the long Georgia season, from November to May, exploring the new course.

MacKenzie died just after the course was completed. He had said, "The Augusta National represented my best opportunity, and I believe my finest achievement." MacKenzie left behind a detailed description of the course and how it might be played. That description can still be used as a guide to the course today, with the footnote that a few holes have since been altered and lengthened, and the original first and second nines were reversed in 1935 (after one Masters tournament had been played) so that hole No. 10, for instance, became No. 1. Here is MacKenzie's description with the holes numbered and distances listed as they are today:

No. 1, White Pine. Par 4. Regular distance, 375 yards. Championship distance, 555 yards. Drops in elevation, 80 feet.

"A drive that is long and straight, skirting a group of trees on the right, will be in a favorable position for the second shot. It is difficult to obtain par figures from any other position."

No. 2, Woodbine. Par 5. Regular distance, 490 yards. Championship distance, 555 yards. Drop in elevation, 80 feet.

"This is an interesting, three-shot hole downhill. Each shot will have to be placed with great accuracy, if par figures are obtained. On the other hand it is quite possible for a powerful and accurate player to reach the green in two shots."

No. 3, Flowering Peach. Par 4. Regular distance, 335 yards.

8

Championship distance, 355 yards. Rise in elevation, 15 feet.

"This green is situated on an interesting natural plateau. The right-hand side is broad. It is easy for anyone to reach the wide portion of the green with their second shot, but difficult to reach the narrow end where the pin will usually be placed."

No. 4, Palm. Par 3. Regular distance, 175 yards. Championship distance, 220 yards. Drop in elevation, 15 feet.

"This is a very similar hole to the famous 11th (Eden) at St. Andrews. There have been scores of attempted copies of this famous hole, but there is none that has the charm and thrill of the original. Most of the copies are failures because of the absence of the subtle and severe slopes which create the excitement of the original hole, and also because the turf is usually so soft that any kind of a sloppy pitch will stop. Previous failures followed by, comparatively speaking, increasing successes may have given us sufficient experience to warrant us in hoping that here at last we may have constructed a hole that will compare favorably with the original."

No. 5, Magnolia. Par 4. Regular distance, 425 yards. Championship distance, 450 yards. Rise in elevation, 17 feet.

"This is a similar type of hole to the famous 17th (Road Hole) at St. Andrews. A group of trees forms a corner of the dog leg, instead of the station master's garden, and the green itself is situated on a similar plateau to its prototype."

No. 6, Juniper. Par 3. Regular distance, 160 yards. Championship distance, 190 yards. Drop in elevation, 28 feet.

"This is similar to the Redan Hole at North Berwick (Scotland), but here, owing to its extreme visibility, lie of the land, and beauty of the surroundings, we have no doubt that we have constructed a much more attractive hole than the original Redan."

No. 7, Pampas. Par 4. Regular distance, 320 yards. Championship distance, 365 yards. Difference in elevation, 0.

"This hole is similar in character to the 18th hole at St. Andrews. There is a deep hollow at the front of the green, which it is necessary to attack at the correct angle for par figures to be obtained."

No. 8, Yellow Jasmine. Par 5. Regular distance, 475 yards. Championship distance, 530 yards. Rise in elevation, 76 feet.

"This is a three-shot hole uphill. A player who is sufficiently long to get up in two will be able to define the positions of the green."

No. 9, Carolina Cherry. Par 4. Regular distance, 395 yards. Championship distance, 420 yards. Drop in elevation, 25 feet.

"This is a hole of the Cape-type played slightly downhill. A long, straight drive will give an easy second up to the green."

No. 10, Camellia. Par 4. Regular distance, 445 yards. Championship distance, 470 yards. Drop in elevation, 102 feet.

"On this downhill hole a long drive over hillocks on the right will land in a level area from which an iron shot can be played to the opening of a large hillside green. This hole embodies the most attractive features of the 13th hole at Cypress Point, California, and the 4th at Alwoodly, one of the best of the British inland links."

No. 11, Dogwood. Par 4. Regular distance, 390 yards. Championship distance, 445 yards. Drop in elevation, 76 feet.

"The green is situated in the bend of a stream. The approach has a marked tilt upward from left to right, so that the farther and more accurately a drive is placed the easier the second shot becomes. This should always be a most fascinating hole. I don't know another quite like it."

No. 12, Golden Bell. Par 3. Regular distance, 130 yards. Championship distance, 155 yards. Drop in elevation, 12 feet.

"This is an interesting pitch shot to a long, narrow green immediately over a stream. The bold player will go for the pin on the right, while the less ambitious will steer for the larger landing space on the left side of the green. There is a steep sandy bank covered with beautiful trees beyond the green."

No. 13, Azalea. Par 5. Regular distance, 455 yards. Championship distance, 475 yards. Difference in elevation, 0.

"This is played along the course of a brook, with the final

10

shot finishing to the green over the stream with a background of a hill slope covered with pine trees. The hole has some of the best golfing features of the 17th hole at Cypress Point, California, and the ideal hole depicted in C.B. MacDonald's book."

No. 14, Chinese Fir. Par 4. Regular distance, 405 yards. Championship distance, 420 yards. Rise in elevation, 90 feet.

"This hole embodies some of the features of the 6th hole at St. Andrews. A long drive slightly to the left of center will give a visible shot to the green. From the right the green is semiblind, obstructed by a large mound in the center of the fairway.

No. 15, Fire Thorn. Par 5. Regular distance, 465 yards. Championship distance, 520 yards. Drop in elevation, 23 feet.

"This is a three-shot hole to most golfers. It is not only an interesting three-shot hole, as one will be maneuvering for position from the tee shot onward, but also a magnificent two-shot hole, as a skillful and courageous player aided by a large hillock on the right, will be able to pull his second shot around to the green. A pond in front of the green provides the penalty for the long player who fails to make a perfect second shot."

No. 16, Redbud. Par 3. Regular distance, 125 yards. Championship distance, 190 yards. Drop in elevation, 10 feet.

"This is a somewhat similar hole over water to the best hole (7th) at Stoke Poges, England. It is probably a better hole than the one at Stoke Poges, as the green is more visible and the background more attractive."

No. 17, Nadina. Par 4. Regular distance, 380 yards. Championship distance, 400 yards. Rise in elevation, 28 feet.

"The construction of the green is somewhat similar to the famous 14th (reversed) at St. Andrews. It will be necessary to attack the green from the right and it will be essential to play a run-up shot, if par figures are desired. We hope to make the turf of such a character that an indifferent pitch will not stop on the green. Until players have learned to play the

11

desired shot this will undoubtedly be one of the most fiercely criticized holes."

No. 18, Holly. Par 4. Regular distance, 395 yards. Championship distance, 420 yards. Rise in elevation, 52 feet.

"The tee shot is played over a valley and a bank, running diagonally from left to right. The longer the drive to the right the easier the second shot, as the approach to the green is bunkered heavily on the left."

The new course embodied the ideals of Jones and Mac-Kenzie. But away from the pine-walled seclusion of Augusta golf was not doing so well. The full force of the depression had settled on the land, and golf was suffering along with every other pursuit that wasn't vital to everyday existence. Luxury country clubs were folding up by the dozens. Others were limping along in hock to the banks, and selling off acres of land to meet their bills. Even the new Augusta National had financial troubles. But contributions from members carried it past these crises.

Tournament golf was in an equally precarious condition. The withdrawal of Jones had left a great void that no one seemed capable of filling. A number of fine professionals were still very active, and with the adoption of a larger size ball and the formal approval by St. Andrews of steel-shafted clubs in 1931, the quality of play was improving. But without Jones the game had lost its great drawing card. No longer would millions of golfers and non-golfers alike bend anxious ears to their radios for word of how "their Bobby" was doing. Attendance sagged badly, and the sponsors of even the U.S. Open and the other major championships were happy when their gate receipts matched their expenses.

At about this time there was considerable feeling within the U.S.G.A. in favor of holding its premier event, the Open, somewhere in the South. The South had never had an Open. It was suggested that the ideal place to hold the tournament would be "Bob Jones's new course in Augusta." Eventually the subject came up for discussion in the old manor house at the end of Magnolia Drive. The members of the Augusta

National were struck by the tournament idea, but the thought of having the U.S.G.A. or any outside group move in and run the tournament on their grounds didn't sit very well. If we are going to have a tournament, they decided, let's do it ourselves and in our own way.

Thus, in brief, the idea for the Masters was born. It would be an invitation affair, a chance for all of Jones's old compatriots and the best of the new players to get together at Bob's place for some good golf and a good time. A single round would be played on each of four days. The past national amateur champions would be invited, along with all the U.S. Open champions, the top twenty-four finishers in the previous year's Open, and other selected players. The date was set for the fourth week in March, 1934, and some eighty-eight invitations went out. Prize money was set at $5,000. The young club had a minimum of capital, so members were induced to donate the prizes. Bartlett Arkell of New York, founder of the Beechnut Company, put up the first prize, $1,500. Jay Monroe of Orange, New Jersey, and Burton Peek of Moline, Illinois, also donated prize money.

With that settled, Tournament Chairman Cliff Roberts turned to his biggest obstacle: convincing Jones to play. "He had made up his mind never to play any more tournament golf," Roberts said later. "I don't think anyone except myself could have prevailed upon him to do it. I couldn't have done it except that I was able to convince him the only way the tournament could be sure of success was by his participation. I pointed out to him that as the host, who planned to invite all his tournament golf pals to come here and play his golf course, he couldn't very well invite them and then refuse to play with them. So, from all angles, Bob was in a position where he had little or no choice except to play—at least for a few years until the tournament became established." Jones finally agreed.

Roberts suggested the name "Masters" tournament, but Jones vetoed this as too presumptuous. So the first tournament was named the Augusta National Invitation. But the word

13

Masters soon found its way into the press, and it caught on immediately. Stories about the first tournament referred to "the Masters," even though it was several years before Jones gave in and agreed to the use of the word in the formal title.

The announcement of the forthcoming tournament was made early in 1934, but all mention of the tourney and the site was lost in the hullabaloo over the companion announcement. It was the most exciting golf news the public had heard in more than three long years: Bobby Jones was coming back!

1934

"JONES TO TEE OFF AT AUGUSTA TODAY," stated
the New York *Times* headline. "Eyes of Golfdom on Southern
Course as Ex-Champion Stages Comeback; Faces Brilliant
Field."

The question that is currently agitating the sports world in
general and this old Southern countryside in particular [wrote
the *Times* correspondent]—Can Bob Jones come back?—will be
answered at least in part tomorrow when the great Georgian
quits handshaking for some earnest club swinging in the first
round of the Masters invitation tournament.

Jones himself was interviewed by an excited band of jour-
nalists, headed by Grantland Rice, himself a member of the
club, and O. B. Keeler, Jones's biographer. Said Bob, "I hope
to be able to step four fast rounds. But I can't even venture
a prediction on what will happen. It looks like a wide open
tournament to me and I hope we will all have a good time."

Jones had set the course record with a practice round of 65, and despite his three-year layoff from competition he was regarded as a co-favorite with Paul Runyan at 6 to 1. Macdonald Smith, Denny Shute, Craig Wood, Horton Smith, and Willie Macfarlane were also rated highly in the choice field of seventy-two professionals and amateurs.

On the eve of the tournament Jones teamed with amateur Ross Sommerville in a Scotch foursome competition. Billy Burke and John Golden won the event with a 32-35-67. Jones and his partner Sommerville could do no better than a 76. Bob was plagued by erratic putting. He was using a duplicate of his Calamity Jane putter, the original of which was then on display in the trophy room of the Royal and Ancient Club at St. Andrews. He had difficulty finding the proper line on the fast greens, and missed several short putts as well. After his round Jones spent a full hour on the practice green, sharp evidence that despite his duties as club president and host he was entering the tournament with serious intent.

Under Chairman Cliff Roberts the complicated arrangements for the tournament had been accomplished with the air of a first-class business operation—despite a small budget. Parking, concessions, player housing (five dollars a day American plan at the Bon Air, four dollars at the Partridge), transportation, crowd marshals, tickets (two dollars per day, five dollars for the full tournament), press facilities, and comfort stations, as well as evening entertainment for the players were provided by a network of committees recruited from the membership.

"The course seems in shape for some explosive scoring," wrote one correspondent. "Par 72 for the 6,700-yard layout has been cracked by at least a dozen men in practice. But the greens are craftily situated. The premium will be on control and putting, which is why Mac Smith and Paul Runyan look like the best bets to give Jones a real battle."

The first Masters round was played Thursday, March 22, 1934. At 10 A.M. Ralph Stonehouse of Indianapolis and Johnny Kinder of Asbury Park sent their drives down the

16

long first fairway. Thirty-five minutes later Jones teed off in a twosome with Runyan. A gallery of one thousand, loyal and confident, followed Jones, while the rest of the field played in virtual privacy. But it was not to be Jones's day. He shot a 76.

As one observer put it, "Four years ago Bobby Jones stood supreme with no more worlds to conquer. Today he came trudging back along the path, buffeted and beaten by the game over which he once reigned as conqueror. Today Bob found the course fighting him, breaking down his putting and his short game."

Jones had brought back to the game all his mastery of the shot from the tee, all his prowess with the brassie and the spoon. The woods were his. But his chip shots to the green and his putting were rusty and awry. He went out in 36, a bit unsteady but pulling through by sheer effort and mechanics. It was at the 11th hole (now No. 2) that the strain began to tell. On this par 5 he hit a perfect brassie from a hanging lie two hundred yards to the green. But he missed his eagle from five feet and almost missed the birdie as well. He three-putted Nos. 14, 17, and 18 to finish with a 40 on the second nine and thirty-five putts in all.

"I know what's wrong," said Jones. "I can't get that putting stroke back and I'm chopping at the chip shots." Then he trudged off to the practice green. The arc of his putting swing had never been a wide one. He always had kept it close to the turf. But now he was lifting the blade higher on the back of his arc. As a result he was batting the ball and pulling his putts to the left. Over refreshments in the clubhouse Macfarlane, Cruickshank and others offered cures for Jones's putting ills.

"It reminds me of a fellow with a bad cold who gets a remedy from all his friends," joked Bob. "I appreciate them all and I hope one will work. Maybe what I need is a square ball."

It was not until late afternoon that the low scores began to come in. The entire field had waited tensely for the challenge of Jones, just as entire fields in a later day would wait for Ben Hogan to make his move. When Jones's 76 was posted in the early afternoon the news spread quickly. Those who were on the course began to improve and those waiting at the starter's tent opened fire with complete relaxation.

Tagging along in the Jones gallery that morning was a lanky young man from Missouri. Horton Smith, age twenty-five, his wavy hair parted in the middle, was a serious fellow who never smoked and who drank nothing stronger than fresh milk. Five years before, Horton Smith had taken the professional golf world by storm. On the 1929 winter tour he won seven of eight tournaments and his $15,000 earnings set a new high. He had a rough-hewn swing and a velvet putting touch. The press dubbed him "Boy Wonder" and "The Joplin Ghost." He was picked as the man most likely to succeed Jones. The 1929 tour was the last before the stock market crash, but that didn't curtail the 1930 jaunt of the pros. Again the winter tour was a Horton Smith benefit. He won $15,500, to set a mark that lasted eight years.

Early in 1930 Smith and Bob Jones were thrown together. "I showed up first in Atlanta, a fresh kid who just wanted to see the place that produced him," Horton was quoted later. "I can't tell you what it meant to a pro to think about Jones. You wanted to beat him, that's what. If you were a pro you wanted to beat Jones."

The two golfers traveled together to the Savannah Open. For Jones it was his first tournament of the year. He was warming up for the big ones to come.

"Bob let me room with him in Savannah," recalled Smith. "We played our two practice rounds together and he introduced me around. But I still wanted to beat him."

Smith did beat his famous roommate in Savannah, 278 to 279. It was the only tournament Jones lost that year. He won the Southeastern Open by fourteen strokes. Smith challenged him in the U.S. Open, but Horton fell back after a bad third round. After the Open, Smith slipped into a discouraging period of playing off form. He was composed and serious, but

18

his golf simply wasn't up to the big matches. He played on the Ryder Cup team in Scotland, picked up polish and a wardrobe of stylish clothes; he progressed mentally and technically, but he didn't win matches. To complicate his troubles he broke his left arm. Finally, after two mediocre years, the slump ended. The pendulum swing that he had developed as a boy, by clipping the heads off dandelions, came back to him, and by 1934 Horton Smith was back in the money.

Horton followed Jones for fourteen holes on the first day at Augusta. "From tee to green he was as good as ever," recalled Smith. "But he wasn't able to concentrate perfectly on the greens as he once had. It was March and those greens were awfully slick. I could tell he was having trouble. Then it was time for me to start my own round."

Smith shot a 70 to tie aging Emmett French of Southern Pines and young Jimmy Hines of Timber Point, Long Island, for the lead. An eagle 3 at No. 17 brought him in two under par. Walter Hagen, playing despite a sprained wrist, had a 71. So did Jimmy Golden, Craig Wood, and Henry Picard. Jones's 76 left him in a tie for thirty-fifth place.

The second day was cold and gloomy and Jones again did little to warm the three thousand fans who dogged his steps. He shot a 74, using thirty-eight putts. Three times he three-putted, the last coming on No. 16, where he missed from just twelve inches away. Said Bob, "Gosh, I was terrible. I was worse today than yesterday."

Horton Smith matched five bogeys with five birdies for even par 72, and took sole possession of the lead at 142. Ed Dudley, the home pro, set a competitive course record with 69 and tied Billy Burke for second place at 143. Wood had 145; Hagen slipped to 147.

Ross Sommerville, the Canadian amateur, produced the first hole in one of the Masters, a 145-yard niblick shot that bounced into the cup on No. 7. (now No. 16). But Sommerville had a 78 for a 160 total.

At 150 Jones was eight strokes off the lead and tied for twenty-eighth position. It was obvious that an old-fashioned

19

Jones comeback would be required to bring him back into the running. Jones decided to change putters. He called his friend Chick Ridley, an Atlanta professional, and described the club he wanted. It was a rusty old model of Calamity Jane, which Jones had given to his mother years before. Ridley found it in her bag of clubs at the East Lake Club and brought it to Augusta. The putter appeared out of place along with Bob's other shiny implements. The head was rusted and the shaft was made of wood. But Jones used it all the way on his third round, and his putting improved. He used only thirty putts, and he matched par 72 for the first time. But 72 was not low enough, and the crowd around him on No. 18 as he dropped his final putt knew it was not enough even as they cheered. Horton Smith was in with 70 for 212, and he now led Jones by ten strokes.

Jones's father, Colonel Robert P. Jones, met Bob at the clubhouse and said, "I congratulate you, son, on that last nine [a 34]."

The strain that had gripped Jones for three days seemed to fade away and he said, "I feel better now, even if I did have to do some wild things to get home."

It was clear Bob Jones was not going to win the first Masters, but still his performance had been remarkable. In eighteenth place he stood ahead of more than fifty of the nation's best professionals and amateurs. A check of the parking lot showed that his comeback had attracted automobiles from thirty states, four from Canada, one from Mexico, and one from Cuba. The interest in his return had given golf a needed boost, and had made the Masters an event of national importance in its first year.

Now the question was, if Jones couldn't win, who would? Smith had the lead, but Burke, the 1931 Open champion, was just one stroke behind him at 213. Dudley and Wood were tied at 214. Runyan had 215 and Hagen 217. Wood had recorded the second 69 of the tournament to get himself back into contention.

The leaders bundled up in sweaters and woollen knickers

for their final round on a crisp March Sunday. Handsome Craig Wood teed off early and promptly plunged into the woods on the 1st hole. His second shot struck a tree and bounded far back into the forest. He hit again, and this time his ball traveled 150 yards to stop a foot from the cup. Craig holed out for his 4. By noon Wood was home with 71-285, a tough standard for the others to shoot at.

Dudley drove into the creek on No. 4 and ruined his chances. Runyan needed a 70 to catch Wood, but a 37 on the first nine slowed him down and he finished with 71, one stroke shy of the lead. Billy Burke clenched his big cigar and strained for extra distance. But fortune turned against him. On the 16th, 17th, and 18th greens his putts hung so close to the lip of the cup that the gallery yelled for him to wait for a breeze to blow the ball in. Each time the ball seemed to be looking down into the cup. The wind blew, but it never seemed to strike the ball. Each time Burke was forced to tap the ball in. He finished with a 73 and 286.

Hagen was teamed with Jones and both played erratically. Walter had 40 going out, Bob 37. Jones rallied to 35 coming in for another 72, but the best Hagen could do was 77. The two old champs tied for thirteenth place at 294, along with Denny Shute.

That left Horton Smith with par to beat Wood. And par he shot. Using a Bobby Jones model driver he had borrowed from Runyan the day before the tournament started, Smith was driving better than ever before in his career. Two holes had bothered him all week, the 9th and 10th. But Horton got past these with a par and a birdie. By the 17th he needed a ten-foot birdie putt on the mountainous green to take the lead. He stroked it in. He came down No. 18 with a tremendous wallop, then pitched twenty-five feet from the pin. His first putt was four feet short, but the next one dropped in, and Horton Smith stood up and grinned.

The one-time "Boy Wonder" had won his first major title, and was the first champion of the Masters. Said Smith, "I feel like I'm back on my game after three years of trying."

Said Bob Jones, "I hope everyone enjoyed himself, and I hope you'll all be back next year."

THE LEADING SCORES:

Horton Smith	284	$1,500
Craig Wood	285	800
Billy Burke	286	550
Paul Runyan	286	550
Ed Dudley	288	400
Willie Macfarlane	291	300
Harold McSpaden	292	175
Al Espinosa	292	175
Jimmy Hines	292	175
Macdonald Smith	292	175
Mortie Dutra	293	100
Al Watrous	293	100
Denny Shute	294	. . .
Robert T. Jones, Jr.	294	. . .
Walter Hagen	294	. . .
		$5,000

In a twilight tableau Dutch Harrison holes his final
putt on the 18th green in the 1954 Masters.

Periscopes and Army uniforms dot the gallery that
banks in a huge horseshoe around the 18th green on
the final afternoon at Augusta.

1935

YOUNG Eugene Sarazen, in a way, had staked his life against the chance of becoming a golf champion. As caddy No. 99 at Apawamis Golf Club in Harrison, New York, he would slip onto the course at sunrise to play a few furtive holes. To the despair of his schoolteachers, Gene's mind was still climbing over the bunkers of Apawamis while he sat uncomfortably indoors the rest of the day. During World War I he had gone to work in an ammunition factory and had contracted empyema. "Find a job in the open air," the doctor had told him, and young Gene knew just the job.

He found a place as assistant clubmaker at Brooklawn in Bridgeport, Connecticut; and soon, showing the first signs of an immense travel lust, he moved on to jobs as assistant professional at Fort Wayne and Titusville, Pennsylvania.

Sarazen was twenty when he clubbed his way to the top of his profession. At Skokie, Illinois, in 1922, playing in his third U.S. Open, Gene trailed the leaders by four strokes as he teed off early on the final round. Unnoticed and unknown,

23

he was under a minimum of pressure. After two shaky holes he decided recklessly to hit out on every shot, to give every putt a chance to drop. On No. 3 his bold forty-footer fell, and on No. 4 he scored from twenty-five feet. On the final hole he used his driver twice to reach the green, then dropped a final birdie for 68-288 and the early lead.

In the clubhouse, congratulations for Sarazen were mixed with a warning: Any one of several players on the course still could beat his 288. "That's possible," conceded the unknown twenty-year-old, "but I've already got mine."

Sarazen's brash finish stood up. Walter Hagen finished at 291, Jones at 289. The kid from Harrison and Titusville was U.S. Open champion. He followed up by winning the P.G.A., then gambled his new reputation by challenging Hagen to a seventy-two-hole match for the unofficial world's championship in 1923. The "Haig" was a man-killer in match play, but the swarthy youngster with the slick black hair and the knickers traded snarl for stare and stroke for stroke. Sarazen won three and two, and his membership with Jones and Hagen in golf's golden circle of the twenties was confirmed.

In the dull years immediately after 1930 Gene Sarazen did more than any other man to keep a flash of color in the struggling game. For the hungry fans he was a lone link with the exciting and heroic twenties. Jones was on the sidelines and Hagen was over the hill. But Sarazen was in action and on the move. Touring the world with a golf bag he attracted galleries from Carnoustie to Sydney and Tokyo with his wicked swing and outgoing manner.

Between rounds he made headlines with his outspoken opinions. "The grip is ninety-five per cent of the game," he said. He advocated replacing the traditional four and a quarter inch cup with one eight inches across, but later conceded he would settle for a six-inch diameter.

Gene once earned ten thousand dollars by winning the first Agua Caliente tournament, then refused to play there again because pari-mutuel betting was permitted.

In 1931, struggling for victories, Sarazen said, "When I get hunches, I win; and I never fail to play a hunch." The next winter, putting his clubmaking experience to personal use, he developed a new club, the sand wedge—a breakthrough that made him the best trap player in the world. The club also made every duffer who ever trickled onto the beach eternally grateful.

In 1932 Sarazen's personal manager, Ray McCarthy, publicly guaranteed Gene a fantastic $250,000 for his services for two years. Then McCarthy promptly made another headline by insuring Gene's health for that same figure, with a $100,-000 policy on Sarazen's hands alone.

At Fresh Meadows, Long Island, in 1932 Gene repeated his Open victory of a decade before. This time he played a cautious, set game for two-and-a-half rounds and was buried in the pack when a deuce on the 45th hole finally inspired him to throw away his governor. Banging every shot hell for leather, Sarazen tore through the final twenty-eight holes in an even hundred strokes for a clean, three-stroke victory.

From Fresh Meadows Sarazen went on to win the British Open championship that had eluded him for so long. The double victory earned him the 1932 Associated Press award as athlete of the year.

The outlook for the 1935 Masters had narrowed to a duel between Sarazen and Bob Jones. After thinking it over for a year, the Jones loyalists decided that Bob had merely needed the inaugural tournament as a warmup in his inevitable comeback. Southern money made him the favorite at 6 to 1.

Sarazen was also making a comeback. Gene had missed the first Masters; he was on an overseas tour in tandem with Joe Kirkwood. He had not won a big tournament in two years. At the P.G.A. in 1933 Tommy Armour, a master with the needle, had spiked Sarazen with one sharp taunt: "We old-timers are washed up, and we don't know it."

Sarazen had won that tournament, but the taunt bothered him. He was only thirty-three in 1935, but perhaps he was an old-timer. It had been a long thirteen years since that first big moment in Skokie. Most of his old comrades were reduced to club golf and token tournament appearances. The gulf between the decades seemed more like a lifetime.

Sarazen went to work early at Augusta. He played four practice rounds in an amazing total of 271—seventeen strokes below par. He shot nothing higher than a 5 on any practice hole, and a handful of reporters on the second-story porch of the clubhouse heard him predict that the man who shot no 6's would win the tournament.

Still the handy money downtown and in the lobby of the Bon Air hotel made Gene, at 7 to 1, second choice behind Jones. Horton Smith, the defender, Paul Runyan, home pro Ed Dudley, Craig Wood, Tommy Armour, and Olin Dutra, the current Open champion, ranged behind them at from 10 to 15 to 1. Jones shot an even par 72 in practice, but the experts were saying his game was still a brassie shot away from the consistency he would need to beat his professional guests.

Sixty-six amateurs and professionals set out opening day in a chilling, gray mist to earn their share of honor and the five-thousand-dollar prize money. By afternoon the sun was shining and a thousand of the home folk turned out to watch them.

The numbering of the first and second nines had been reversed since the inaugural Masters, so that hole No. 10 now became No. 1, No. 11 became No. 2, and so on.

Henry Picard, playing out of Hershey, Pennsylvania, took the first lap lead with a 67. Picard had been leading money winner on the winter circuit, and his exploits had earned him the monicker of "Hershey Hurricane." His 67 lowered the competitive course record by two strokes, but it earned him no more than a one-stroke lead over three challengers. One was Willie Goggin, who had used a six iron to sink a hole in one on the 16th hole. The second was Ray Mangrum. Sarazen, who had played one of the sparkling rounds of his career, was the third. Only failure to drop four putts, ranging from three to six feet, had kept Sarazen as high as 68. Jones, meanwhile, had required 74, and the odds on Sarazen dropped with a thump to 3½ to 1.

The following day Bob Jones forced memories back five years as, for the first time since his retirement, he demonstrated the championship skill that made him a legend. He electrified the crowd with a front nine 33—three strokes under par—and the uneasy message reached other players on the course. Bobby was back. But just as quickly as he had found it, Jones lost his putting touch again on the back nine. He slumped to a 39-72 and an inglorious tie for eighteenth place. Over a glass in the clubhouse later he admitted wryly, "Maybe I'm just a nine-hole golfer."

Picard kept his lead with a 68 for a fancy 135. Sarazen was four back at 139.

On Saturday only half a thousand ventured out in the blustery rainstorms that swept the Augusta National course. Picard, the winter champion, teed off at the height of the storm. The first nine holes ruined him. He sloshed home in 76 and was never again a factor.

Rangy Craig Wood proved himself the mud horse of the day. On the 525-yard 2nd hole he was the only man in the field to get home in two against the wind. From that point he put together six birdies and a 68. At 209 he stood one stroke up on Dutra and three up on Sarazen. Jones had a respectable but uninspired 73, ten strokes back.

Wood teed off some four holes ahead of Sarazen on the wintry final day. He started poorly. Accurate putts saved him on three of the first four holes, but he three-putted the 5th, missed the green on the short 6th, and turned in 39. Sarazen, playing steadily, drew even with Wood after eight holes. But a drive into the rough followed by a wide approach cost him a bogey five at No. 9.

Wood, playing No. 15, earned his bird with two good woods to the green. Another birdie at 18 set off a cheer from the gallery that reached Sarazen and his partner, the venerable Hagen, on No. 14.

The "Haig" shook his head and said, "Well, Gene, it looks like it's all over."

Sarazen, now three strokes down with only five holes to

27

play, bristled back, "I dunno. They could drop in from any-where."

Sarazen turned away from his ball in the wet fairway grass and peered down the long slope to the 15th green, 220 yards away. A freezing wind disturbed the flag and rippled through his protective sweater. Around him, one thousand eyewit-nesses huddled together in a crescent that bulged behind the green and thinned out to a single line on either side of the fairway.

Before the green lay a pond. Not much of a pond, really, perhaps forty feet across at its broadest. It protected the green about as well as a moat protects a castle. This particular moat served its purpose in the Bob Jones design for par-five holes. It discouraged the faint-hearted and penalized the foolhardy. Yet it was no obstacle on the road to an easy birdie for the player who could put two excellent wood shots together and was willing to gamble.

Gene Sarazen was that gambler. He reached for his favored four wood, took another quick glimpse ahead through the mist, and swung away.

He watched his ball as best he could as it sailed up into the haze and over the moat to the 15th green. It dropped on the apron, popped up twice on the turf, and rolled steadily toward the cup as though homing on a magnet. A thousand voices in the gallery screamed as the ball disappeared into the cup for a double eagle 2.

Gene Sarazen strode down the remaining two hundred yards of fairway between the two lines of shouting fans like a king walking to his throne—the four wood held in front of him like a scepter. "I started figuring," said the man who had not cared much for schoolboy arithmetic long ago, "and it was the greatest thrill I have ever had on a golf course. I realized all I needed was par to tie."

Par was exactly what Sarazen got on the final three holes to confirm his tie with Wood, and in effect clinch the tourna-ment. Craig, who had stood with his wife in the clubhouse receiving congratulations when the fateful roar from 15 reached him, never quite recovered from the nerve shock of that dismal message. One reporter likened him to a bettor who had drawn a sweepstakes winner but had lost his ticket on the way to the pay-off window.

Next morning a sparse four hundred were in attendance when Sarazen and Wood teed off for their thirty-six-hole play off over a waterlogged course. Like most play offs, this one was anticlimactic. Wood led twice on the front nine, but they turned even. Wood had no confidence in his putter. Eight times he was short on putts that might easily have dropped, if he had given them more legs. Sarazen, meanwhile, working coolly with his center-shafted putter, was 7 under twos on the thirty-six greens.

Wood was consistently longer off the tees. Ironically, this worked against him. Shooting first, Sarazen, who had learned his gamesmanship in bitter combat against Hagen, would stiffen his approach shot to the pin, then turn to his opponent with a look that meant, "See if you can trump that." Wood rarely could.

Sarazen moved ahead on No. 10 with a twenty-footer for his birdie 3. Wood missed his approach on 11 and bogeyed the hole. On No. 12, while Gene gathered an easy par, Wood putted twice from six feet for a bogey 4. The 13th played its inevitable part. Wood drove into the left-hand creek. He dropped out, tried desperately for the green, and hooked again into the creek. He dropped out again, pitched on, and sank a six-footer for a 6. Sarazen played safe for his par 5. Over Jones's "fateful four" first holes on the back nine Sarazen had built a four-stroke lead. From there in he played like a machine, parring twenty-four straight holes from No. 11 through No. 34.

Sarazen turned in 71 with his four-stroke lead intact, and at the end he had won the play off by a full 5, 144 to 149. Prophetically, he had played the one hundred eight holes without taking a 6.

For Sarazen the winner's purse was $1,500; for Wood, $800. Unprincely rewards even for 1935. Far more lasting was the effect of Sarazen's epic shot with the four wood. The fledgling Masters in its second year had produced the most dramatic single shot ever executed in golf, before or since. The tournament had its first tradition. And Jones, who had finished well back among the mortals at 297, could see with satisfaction that his course and his tournament had stepped forward to stand on their own, while he himself retreated happily closer to the background.

1936

NINETEEN THIRTY-SIX was the year golf turned the corner. The number of member clubs in the U.S.G.A., reduced by fatalities from 1,154 in 1931 to 767 in 1935, had finally leveled off. In 1936 the number actually started upward. Fred Corcoran was hired as tournament director of the pro circuit, and for the first time total purses hit $100,000. For the professionals the jackpot was starting to sweeten a little. Not even Corcoran dreamed how sugary it was to become in the next twenty-five years.

In Augusta the third Masters was destined to be plagued by weather—black, bad weather. But there was no advance warning of that, as each practice day produced a bright new headline. Bob Jones shot a 64, a course record, and his loyalists did heart flips again. The odds on Jones opened at 8 to 1. He shot four sub-par practice rounds in 274. The odds dropped to 6 to 1, even though he hadn't played a tournament in a year. Defending champion Sarazen could be had at 8 to 1, and Horton Smith, who had won in 1934, was no better than 11 to 1.

On Wednesday amateur champion Lawson Little declared he was turning professional. The sturdy, slugging Little, twenty-five and just married, had been promised ten thousand dollars to make exhibitions and a movie. "You can't support a wife on gold medals," he told reporters in the clubhouse.

Torrential rains killed Thursday's opening round, and the field fretted indoors. On Friday the masters finally teed off in freezing temperatures and a blustery wind that cut through two and three thicknesses of sweater. Fingers stiffened around the club grips. Craig Wood, already twice a bridesmaid, blew to an 88. He was out of it fast this time, despite a closing 67, 69, 76. Sarazen reached "his" hole, No. 15, took a bogey 6 and finished with 78. Jones's comeback came a cropper with a 78.

Only Harry Cooper, "Light Horse Harry" from Chicago, could better par. He had a 70 and Jones, back at his hosting duties in the clubhouse, commented, "Conditions today made this course at least six strokes harder than it ordinarily is. So put down Cooper's round as one of the greatest that has ever been played."

Al Espinosa held second place at 72 and Horton Smith lay third with 74. On Saturday the wind died. Sarazen, with a birdie 4 on No. 15, tied the competitive course record with a 67 and moved into a fourth-place tie with Smith. But Cooper shot a 69 to lead his closest rivals, Cruickshank and Denny Shute, by a comfortable five strokes.

Thirty-six holes were scheduled for Sunday, but a downpour postponed the climax another day. Cooper sweated indoors, his five-stroke lead less comfortable now, while a mile away on No. 12 the footbridge over Rae's Creek disappeared under water.

There was no postponement Monday. Two full rounds were played in perhaps the worst weather the Masters has ever known. The rain started about noon. For a while it looked as if the fourth round must be called off, but just before several holes went completely under water the rain stopped. When the field finally went out for the last eighteen, they met the tail end of a hurricane. Black skies frightened the spectators off the course, and more than one golfer felt like running after them. The greens were awash. Grantland Rice called them "as treacherous as a coral snake." It was an unlikely setting for heroics.

Casualties ran heavy. Cruickshank went over par on four of the first five holes on the third round and was lost. Shute fell apart after a good start and slipped to 75. Jones, caught at the height of the storm, finished with a fourth round 77 and a miserable 306, thirty-two strokes higher than his practice total.

That left Cooper, Smith, and Sarazen, as Lawson Little described them later, "trying to crowd through a needle's eye." Cooper managed a morning 71 for a lead of three strokes over Smith and seven over Sarazen.

But on the final round the combined strain of waiting, weather, and winning took its toll on Cooper. Playing through a gale and a cloudburst, Light Horse Harry turned in 39. He started home with seven straight pars, but on 17 he pushed his drive, took a bogey five for a 76-286.

A moving spectator cost Sarazen a third putt and a 6 on the 2nd hole. But at 9 he was even par and had gained three strokes on Cooper.

Sarazen finished gallantly in 70-287. He predicted a 34 for himself coming home, and he got it. But without another miracle on No. 15 he was one stroke short of Cooper.

That left only Smith for Harry to worry over in the clubhouse, and Horton was hot. More accurately, his putter was hot. With his familiar smooth stroke he was putting just as brilliantly through running water as he might have under ideal conditions. Smith himself called it his "magic-wand" style, and in the morning the wand got him a 68.

Playing his final round late, Smith and his partner, Little, got a fortunate break in the weather. The wind calmed and the rain stopped. Still, Smith bogeyed No. 10, when he had to chip all the way to the cup across a flooded green. With five soggy holes to play, the Missouri milk-drinker needed one birdie to tie, two to win.

He got the first at No. 14, holing out with a splash from forty-three feet away. He got the second at 15.

"As I came up to play my second shot," Smith recalled later, "I kept thinking of what Sarazen had done in '35. I had no idea I could put the ball in the hole, but I had the notion firmly fixed in my mind that this was the winning hole. So I took out my own four wood, like Sarazen, and I went for the green."

For a Taft conservative like Smith this was a desperate venture. Said his partner, Little, "I winced to see him take a wood and bang valiantly for the green. He was imbedded in a muddy lie. It was the kind of gamble that makes champions, and the gods were with him. He landed over the pond, forty yards short of the pin, and got down in two for his bird. "Me? I tried the same thing and wound up with a seven."

Smith had one final scare on 17, where his long approach putt skidded sixteen feet past the cup. But he rapped the second putt in, the ball slinging water like an old mill wheel. The Joplin Ghost parred in for his 72-285 and a one-stroke victory just before the rains came again.

The Masters had its first two-time winner in Horton Smith and another classic loser. The disheartened Cooper turned to his host and said, "It seems it wasn't intended for me to win a major tournament."

He was right.

1937

THE 12th green on the National course, about a mile from the shelter of the clubhouse, is planted in the farthest corner of the old plantation—some have called it and the 13th hole Amen Corner. A row of soldierly pines separates the green from the adjoining Augusta Country Club.

The putting surface is long and quite narrow, as judged from the tee 155 yards away. In front of the green and separated from it only by a short, steep bank flows Rae's Creek. Both green and creek fall sharply away to the right. A gusty cross wind makes the delicate tee shot even more tender. When the pin is placed near the narrow right tip of the green the player who decides to go for the flag knows he faces two extremes: a short putt for a deuce, or disaster.

The pin, naturally, was nestled in the far right-hand corner when Ralph Guldahl reached the 12th tee on the final day in 1937. Guldahl, naturally, decided to shoot for the cup. This burly twenty-five-year-old Texan was basically a conservative, but he was also at the top of his game. He had been a professional for nine years and was on the threshold of a two-year period in which he was to dominate golf as no man had done since 1930. Guldahl's first U.S. Open championship lay just two months ahead, with another to follow in 1938. The first of three straight Western Opens was already in his bag.

Guldahl was home free in this 1937 Masters. He had taken command the day before with a third-round 68 that included a brilliant 32 on the back nine. Now he was on the friendly back nine again with a four-stroke lead and seven holes to play. Ed Dudley, the home professional who had started the day in second place, had strayed into the woods on No. 2, taken a 7, and lost his chance. Guldahl, meanwhile, was playing confident, winning golf. He turned in 38. On the 10th he made a superb approach that left him less than a yard from the hole and he earned a birdie 3. He got his par 4 on No. 11.

On the 12th tee Ralph stooped his two hundred pounds over the ball, ignored the fat, left-hand portion of the green, and swung for the flagpole on the right.

But the ball faded a shade to the right as it descended, and a shade was all it took. One foot more and Guldahl would have been putting for a 2. As it was the ball hit near the top of the bank and dropped back into the creek. He took a penalty stroke and dropped a new ball. His third shot was a trifle strong and went over into the grassy dip behind the green. From there he got down in two for a 5—double bogey. It was a bad error, but no one, including Guldahl, thought it would cost him the tournament.

If his experience on No. 12 had shaken up Guldahl at all, his drive on No. 13 did not show it. The 13th tee (until it was moved in 1956) lay five yards to the right and three yards ahead of where it does now. So the dog-leg bend to the left, halfway down the 470-yard fairway, was less acute. The brook, of course, still wound its skinny way past the woods for the full left-hand length of the fairway and cut across the fairway in a mean ditch just before the green. But from the old tee a golfer could play well away from the trouble on the left.

Usually his drive would kick nicely off the banked right side of the fairway and bounce around the corner.

Guldahl's drive did just that, and he found himself a strong four iron away from the green. Careful Ralph chose a three iron to be sure. But he missed his shot and sent the ball spinning again into the ditch. Dropping a new ball, he pitched on and took two putts for a bogey 6. Guldahl had required eleven strokes—three over par—to play Nos. 12 and 13. He parred in from there for a 76-285 and a one-stroke lead over Ed Dudley.

Playing behind Guldahl that first Sunday afternoon in April was John Byron Nelson, Jr. Like Guldahl, Nelson was a touring Texan—Ralph from Dallas, Byron from Fort Worth. Like Guldahl, Nelson had recently turned twenty-five. But unlike Guldahl, Nelson was not well known. He had been a professional barely five years, and in his rookie year, 1932, he had almost starved to death on tournament winnings of nine hundred dollars. It wasn't until 1934, with a stake borrowed from his prospective father-in-law, that Byron had been able to return to the tour and make it stick. He had recently signed on with the Reading, Pennsylvania, Country Club.

This was Nelson's third Masters, but the most notable tournament victory listed behind his name was the 1936 New York Metropolitan. The amiable, moon-faced Texan had a long and loose-jointed "caddy's" swing. And well he might; as a teen-ager Nelson had been a seventy-five-cents-a-round caddy at Glen Garden in Fort Worth. A member there had given him his first club, an old mashie.

Nelson now was in the process of developing a perfectly controlled swing—easy flowing action with a very straight left arm—that was to make him remarkably accurate with woods and long irons. Later they were to call him the "Mechanical Man," but now he was still just an ex-railroad clerk from Texas.

As a boy Nelson had religiously practiced putting, aiming at a folded white handkerchief when it got too dark for him to see the regular hole. But in 1931 he had lost an amateur tournament in Fort Worth, when he missed a three-foot putt on the final hole. Somebody said, "He can't stand pressure."

Now the same charge was up for discussion again. Horton Smith, the defender, Harry Cooper, and Ed Dudley were the bettors' choices in the field of thirty-nine pros and eight amateurs who had teed off in this fourth Masters. For the first time Bob Jones was not among the favorites. He was bunched at 14 to 1 with Guldahl, Nelson, and a rugged-looking newcomer, not yet twenty-five and only recently separated from Bath County, Virginia, Samuel J. Snead.

Jones played himself out of contention with an opening 79. Smith had had his days at Augusta and Snead's were yet to come. Cooper and Dudley were always close, never in.

On opening day Byron Nelson took the Masters lead with a competitive course record of 66. Nelson's round included seven birdies, six one-putt greens. He drove the 340-yard 7th, got home in two on the five-hundred-yard uphill 8th, and sank a six-footer on 9, for a pretty string of three birdies. Guldahl was three strokes back at 69.

On the second day Nelson's mechanical even-par 72 was good enough to keep three strokes of daylight between himself and Guldahl. But after clutching the lead for forty-eight hours, Nelson's putter went haywire on Saturday. On the 4th hole he missed a four-footer. On the 5th he four-putted from within twenty feet. On No. 7 he needed three putts from the back edge. In all, Nelson putted thirty-nine times, and it was considered a small miracle that he made it home in 75. He had lost seven strokes to Guldahl and now trailed him by four.

After each had played eleven holes on Sunday Nelson still trailed by four. Like Guldahl he had covered the first nine in 38. Like Guldahl he had birdied No. 10 and parred No. 11. Like Guldahl he went for the cup on No. 12.

At this point the gaunt and still hungry-looking Nelson became a champion. His tee shot sailed true to the 12th green and he stroked in a ten-foot putt for a birdie 2. On No. 13 his soundly hit approach caught the roll of the green just right and stopped eight feet from the pin. Nelson made it good for an eagle 3. He had played the two holes of Amen Corner in five strokes—six fewer than Guldahl. Nelson had gone from four down to two up in two fateful holes.

The Masters could boast another memorable finish; not as dramatic as Sarazen's one-shot triumph in 1935, but just as effective.

When the unrattled Nelson parred his last five holes for a 70-283 and a clean two-stroke margin over Guldahl the tournament had produced its first "home-grown" Master. Smith and Sarazen had been champions before the National course was built. But Nelson, who had done little enough before, now had won his first major title. In the next ten years he was to compile an unmatched string of personal triumphs.

Nelson's romance with the Masters has blossomed with time. He had played in eighty-six consecutive rounds, when illness forced him to withdraw after the opening round in 1959. He was back in 1960. Nelson won his second Masters in a historic play off with Ben Hogan in 1942. After illness forced Bob Jones to the sidelines in 1949, Nelson replaced him as official "host player" for Masters week at the National course. For several years he was paired with the leader on the final day. He has become a symbol of the tournament.

1938

WALTER HAGEN turned his back to the bar, eyed his audience, and pointed his glass at a young man sitting across the room.

"Henry Picard," said Hagen, "is the coming golfer of this country. He is the pick of the pack. I've never seen a veteran with more poise than that kid."

Then Hagen crossed the room and sat down next to the tanned youngster. For an hour they conversed. Hagen talked, Picard listened.

"You can become one of the great golfers in the world," insisted The "Haig." "Just keep working. And don't try to hit the ball so hard. Why, one of these days you'll make the Ryder Cup."

The public praise and private advice were the honest words of a good sport. An hour before, Picard had given Hagen one of the beatings of his life. In a man-to-man play off for the 1932 Carolina Open Championship at Starmount Country Club Picard had defeated Hagen by ten strokes.

For the tall, taciturn New Englander it was his first notable victory. For Hagen it was the first time in a long career he had ever lost a play off.

On April 1, 1938, Henry Picard's left thumb hurt. He had jammed it painfully a week before, and now as he swung his driver the fluid, effortless rhythm that had become his trademark wasn't quite there. The tender digit was disconcerting. So on almost the eve of the fifth Masters Picard changed his grip from the popular overlapping style to the old-fashioned interlocking. By entwining his left index finger and his right little finger he put more pressure on these two sound digits and less on the sore thumb.

In the years since that conversation with Hagen, Picard had become an established tournament player. Friendly and modest off the course, he still tore into a golf ball as though he hated it. During one long stretch he played even par or better in fifty of fifty-four tournaments. His fellow pros had voted him the best man in the game with full irons. By now it was Picard, the successful veteran, who was giving advice and encouragement, and offering loans to dozens of struggling youngsters. Among them were Ben Hogan, who was at Augusta for his first Masters, and Sam Snead, who had won his first important tournament at Oakland in January and had gone on to turn the winter circuit on its ear.

In 1935 Picard had spread-eagled the field with 67-68 in the first two rounds of the Masters. Then he had tumbled to 76-75 and fourth place behind Sarazen. He had never won a major title.

On the eve of the 1938 Masters Ed Dudley stood in his pro shop and warned the sports writers, "That young Snead will be plenty tough for the boys."

But the opening day's play was rained out before half the field of forty-four could tee off. When the first round was finally played on Saturday hard luck Harry Cooper, to the surprise of no one, was in front with a handsome 68. To the surprise of everyone new sensation Sam Snead shot a 78, with a wild 44 on the second nine. Said Sam, "That was the worst round of golf I've ever played." Henry Picard had an inconspicuous 71.

A double round on Sunday did little toward producing a winner. One leader after another nose-dived. Cooper, to the surprise of no one, lost his lead in the morning. Harry just couldn't seem to pull the right club out of his bag; poor judgment cost him shot after shot. Even after playing the final four holes one under par he slumped in at 77.

After two rounds the leader was Dudley with 139. In the afternoon the home pro went out in 36. Then his game curdled. From No. 10 on he didn't par a hole, his card showing seven bogeys and two birdies for a total of 77. Gene Sarazen put together the best two rounds of the tournament, 70-68. But he had opened with a 78 on Saturday and his 216 total for fifty-four holes left him in a four-way tie with Cooper, Dudley, and Ralph Guldahl, the U.S. Open champ. One stroke up on them and leading the pack for the first time was Picard. Henry had added a pair of 72's to his opening 71, finishing each of his three rounds powerfully with a birdie deuce on 16, birdie trey on 17, and par four on 18.

Picard teed off last among the contenders on Monday's final round. From that vantage point the grapevine kept him informed as the opposition wriggled and died in front of him. Sarazen blew to a 79 and growled in disgust, "I could have kicked the ball around in less than that." Nobody argued the point.

Dudley found the trees on No. 2 again, finished the hole in 6, and was gone. Cooper held his own with par, but no better. Byron Nelson, the defender, started the day two strokes back, but lost three more on the first nine.

Guldahl started brilliantly with a par, eagle, birdie. He turned in 34 and birdied No. 15. But on the 16th Ralph three-putted, and when he did it again on No. 18 he finished in a tie with Cooper, each with 71-287.

Picard, meanwhile, had built himself a sturdy lead with a four-under-par 32 on the front side—sore thumb, new grip, and all. Approaching and putting marvelously, he had started out birdie, birdie. He added two more birds at 7 and 8.

On the final nine Picard's lone duty was to avoid complete collapse. This he did and no more. Twice he three-putted for bogeys. Playing cautiously on treacherous No. 13 he almost took a 6, but his putter saved him. The trusty mallet-head weapon saved him again on Nos. 16 and 17, when his irons left him miles wide of the mark.

By 18 Picard needed only a bogey 5 to win. Instead he sank his final four-footer for a par and a two-stroke victory at 70-285. It was Henry Picard's year.

1939

RALPH GULDAHL, the depression champion, stepped back from his ball on the 10th green, fished a small comb out of his pocket, and while the biggest gallery in Masters history waited, combed his hair.

"Guldahl isn't a golfer," one of his partners had complained, "he's a surveyor."

In that sense Guldahl might be called the Middlecoff of the thirties. Shambling thoughtfully down the fairways he would take his stance four or five times, fiddle, and wipe his hands before hitting a key shot.

"I don't waste any time sizing up the line, choosing a club, or fiddling with my grip once I reach the ball," Guldahl defended himself. "But I try to steady my nerves and slow down my breathing before I take my stance. Combing my hair is part of the plan. That little pocket comb has saved me many a stabbed putt."

"If Guldahl gave someone a blood transfusion the patient would freeze to death," Sam Snead was quoted.

"The truth is that behind my so-called poker face I'm burning up," answered Guldahl. "I know they call me 'the dumb Swede,' and they say I've got no imagination, that I don't know enough to worry about a golf title. I do know that all that matters in golf is the next shot. Maybe the 'dumb' reputation helps me. The others are likely to start pressing if they think I'm not worrying. My wife could tell them different."

"Guldahl is the most underrated golfer I've ever known," said Tommy Armour. "He has everything Jones and Hagen had—except color."

"It was all very well for the others to gather in the locker room after a round and laugh and tell stories and have a few drinks," wrote Grantland Rice, "but Ralph had no laughter in him and no money for drinks. His only thoughts were where to get money to get himself and his family to the next stop on the circuit, if he didn't finish high enough in the money in this one."

"I know what it is to be hungry," confirmed Guldahl.

In 1928 the big Norwegian from Dallas turned professional, before he was seventeen. In the 1933 U.S. Open at North Shore in Chicago young Guldahl gained nine strokes in nine holes on Johnny Goodman, only to miss a tie when he blew a four-foot putt on the final green. After that near-miss at fame Guldahl slipped back into obscurity with his wife and their baby son. For the next three years, like many another depression father, Guldahl wore the same suit of clothes. He squeezed every dime in order to feed his family, stayed in rooming houses while others stayed in hotels, and piled his family on the bus between tournament towns while others drove or rode on trains.

A budget cutback cost him his job as a club pro in St. Louis. At one point he tried to sell automobiles. He sold just one—to himself. After the 1935 Open the Guldahls went home to Dallas broke. Ralph put his family in the new car and headed for California. He played poorly in a few local tournaments. Then, with both his wife and son down sick, he gave up and went to work as a carpenter's assistant at a movie studio. His 1935 tournament earnings had added up to fifty-four dollars: fifty dollars in the Los Angeles Open and four dollars in the Riverside pro-amateur.

By the spring of 1936 Guldahl's golf clubs were in hock. But his wife and some better-heeled friends to whom he had been giving lessons urged him to return to the game. He borrowed money to unhock the clubs and traveled to Detroit for the True Temper Open. A gritty sixth place there earned him $245. Then another friend staked him to new clubs and a new suit and shoes, and Ralph went off to Davenport for the Western Open. With a 64 on the final day Guldahl took the Western title out of Ray Mangrum's clutch, and that was the turning point.

From there Ralph went on to win the old Radix Cup for 1936, with a medal average of 71.63, a record low. (A year before he had finished forty-fifth in the same competition.) That winter he won the Miami-Biltmore and the Atlanta Open, while baby-sitting in his rooming house between rounds. He finished second to Nelson in the 1937 Masters. In the 1937 U.S. Open at Oakland Hills Guldahl overhauled Sam Snead with a final round of 69 and a record 281.

Standing on the final tee at Oakland Hills and needing only a bogey 6 to win, Guldahl had repeatedly stepped away from his ball, wiped his hands on soiled trousers, and peered at the murderous rough on his left. After five minutes of this he asked his partner, Harry Cooper, what he should do. Answered Cooper, "Just don't drop dead." Guldahl got his par.

Sam Snead, making his first run at the Open, had owned the gallery. Blessed with a powerful and perfect swing and abundant natural appeal Sam was the people's choice, the hero everyone had been looking for since Jones retired. But Guldahl won the National championship, and Snead was never to have it.

In 1938 Ralph became the fourth man in history to win two consecutive Opens. He picked up ten strokes on Dick Metz on the final round to win by six. Five days later, in a triumphal return to St. Louis, the somber Norwegian became the first man in history to win the Western three times running, finishing in 65 strokes on the final day at Westwood. The Guldahls, with two boys in the family by now, had paid off their debts, and by the modest standards of 1938 they were in the money.

It was Snead against Guldahl again in the Masters of 1939. The first day's play was washed out and rescheduled for a final 36 holes on Sunday. Tough little Billy Burke, bracketed with Jones at odds of 40 to 1, aroused the long-shot players with a first-round score of 69. Snead was one back at 70. Guldahl had 72.

The next day Gene Sarazen shot a 66 in a hailstorm to tie the tournament record and lead by a stroke after 36 holes. Gene, who could be counted on to electrify the crowd one way or another, had started off in a stiff breeze that finally brought pelting rain and hailstones "as large as robins' eggs." He never strayed from the fairway, and his putter was hot. Guldahl's and Snead's were not. They tied for second at 140, one stroke behind Sarazen.

The sun came out for Sunday's double round, and eight thousand spectators streamed onto the National grounds— more than had ever seen a Masters before. Unlike earlier galleries, which came mostly for a glimpse of Bob Jones, the eight thousand were drawn by the promise of another memorable Masters finish.

After the morning round six leaders were blanketed. Guldahl with 70-210 clutched a one-stroke lead over Sarazen. Snead, Burke, Little, and Nelson were bunched at 212.

In the afternoon Burke was first to round the turn with a 37, which proved to be too high. Nelson came to the 10th with a 39 and was finished. Sarazen could do no better than par, and that wasn't good enough, either.

By the time Guldahl reached the turn Sam Snead had holed out on the near-by 18th green with a brilliant 68. Sam had established a new Masters record of 280 for four rounds.

Guldahl had played the first nine in even par 36, and as

the big gallery cut away from Snead on the 18th green to follow Guldahl down the 10th fairway Ralph knew exactly what he had to do. A two under par 34 would tie Snead. A 33 would win.

On the 10th green Guldahl put the little comb back in his pocket, stood up to his ball, and stroked it in for a birdie 3. Lawson Little, playing with Guldahl and tied with him after nine holes, missed a three-foot putt and fell two strokes back with a bogey 5.

Guldahl parred No. 11, his birdie putt lacking six inches. Now he stood again on the 12th tee, where a missed shot had started his crash twenty-four months before. This time Guldahl pitched firmly to within six feet of the flag, missed his putt, but got his par 3.

That brought No. 13. Guldahl's drive was weak. It stopped on the sharp slope of the fairway, 220 yards from the tee. In order to get home in two—and every greenhorn in the crowd knew he must do this to catch Snead—he needed a terrific carry of 230 yards to clear the ravine that housed the brook. Guldahl had been that route before. Now he chose his No. 3 spoon, clubbed the ball from its side-hill lie, and watched it whistle home and come to rest six feet from the cup. It was the shot of a master, and it won the tournament. Guldahl's gamble was rewarded a moment later when he holed a curling putt for an eagle 3. In four holes he had caught Snead and passed him.

Par in would win for Guldahl, and he got it. On the final hole a perfectly placed drive to the right-hand side of the fairway left him with a three iron shot up "heartbreak hill." He was a little strong, but the ball held on the back edge. He lobbed back to within a foot. This time Guldahl left his comb in his pocket, as he tapped in the putt that made him a winner.

Snead's 280 had pushed Guldahl to 279, a standard that was not to be lowered until Ben Hogan's perfect tournament fourteen years later.

48

1940

ONCE upon a time, in the not so long ago, if you cut any ice with a golf club, you had to come from Texas—unless, of course, your name was Sam Snead.

The Texans swarmed in with a daring, long-clouting brand of golf, and dominated the game for the better part of two decades. The Lone Star travelers had courage and color. They snapped scoring records, grabbed off every championship in sight, and went home to Texas lugging bags of Yankee gold.

Some said their secret lay in the mild Texas weather, which allowed them to play around the calendar while young players in the North were sitting out the winter. Some said their secret lay in the miserable Texas weather, which taught them to play in high winds and to adjust to sudden changes. Some pointed out that almost all of them came up by the same route—from hungry young caddy to hungrier young pro to champion.

Whatever the reason, they set a pace that only one man

could match: Sam Snead, the muscular slugger from Bath County, Virginia, by way of White Sulphur Springs. And there were those who swore Sam just had to have some Texas blood in his veins somewhere.

From the end of the thirties to the middle fifties the Texans with Snead won eleven Masters championships out of a possible fifteen and produced the runner-up in three of the other four years. Over the same period the Texans (without Snead) won eight of a possible thirteen National Opens.

It was during the era of the Texans that American golf pulled out of the doldrums of the post-Jones years, and reached up for a new stature that all but eclipsed the memories of the Golden Twenties. Each year more men and women played golf, and more players of exceptional quality appeared on the tournament circuit. Each year more citizens flocked to watch the champions play, and each year the pot of gold for the winners multiplied.

Fittingly enough it was the Masters that the Texans, with Snead, chose as the battleground for some of their most spectacular performances and bitterest intramural showdowns. The young tournament felt their presence early. Byron Nelson of Fort Worth had won in 1937. Ralph Guldahl of Dallas held forth in 1939, but it was in 1940 that the Texans took over in force. And their way of doing it left no doubt in anyone's mind that Sam Houston's boys were here to stay.

The strongest field so far assembled teed off on the first day of the seventh Masters in 1940. All five previous champions were on hand. So were a fine set of bridesmaids: Ed Dudley, Harry Cooper, Craig Wood, Paul Runyan, and Lawson Little. Bob Jones had played twenty-seven practice holes in one hundred strokes, eight under par. Sam Snead was in form, as were the two Texans who had dominated the winter circuit, Ben Hogan and James Newton Demaret. Amateur Charles Yates fired a practice 68. Last man invited to join the swank field was Lloyd Mangrum, one of the golfing Mangrum brothers of Dallas, and recent winner of the Thomasville, Georgia, Open. Guldahl and Hogan were co-favored at 6 to 1,

50

and Nelson and Demaret were not far behind. Opening day dawned clear and windy.

Apple-cheeked Jimmy Demaret had descended upon an unprepared public three months before. A product of the caddy yard—he was appointed caddy master at age ten— Demaret had been cutting his teeth on the circuit for six seasons without particular success, except at making friends. Those who watched his cheerful nonchalance on the course and his ability to relax afterward said, "He must have been tutored by Hagen himself." Those who were blinded by his predilection for courageous combinations of brilliantly colored clothes compared him to "two rainbows competing for first place in a color contest." Jimmy wore shoes and trousers in hues that never were meant for shoes and trousers. In the evening he switched to high-heeled Texas boots. With the broad horizontal stripes of his shirts he resembled a fugitive from a Georgia chain gang. He also wore a soft green felt "lucky" hat turned rakishly down over his left ear.

In a streak that started in January Demaret won five tournaments at Oakland, San Francisco, Houston (the Western Open), New Orleans, and St. Petersburg. By April his earnings ($6,000) were already as much as the leading money winner could make in a year a few seasons earlier. Jimmy's happy-go-lucky attitude became big news.

On the final green at St. Petersburg Byron Nelson had canned a birdie putt and left Demaret needing a four-footer to win. While the gallery tensed, Demaret sauntered up to his ball, smiled at it in mock tenderness, looked up at the crowd, and chirped, "Would anyone like to sink this one for me?" While the gallery chuckled, Jimmy sank his own putt.

Invited to his first Masters in 1939, Demaret had finished tied with Bob Jones in thirty-third place—out of the money. Teamed with Jones in a 1940 practice round, Jimmy joshed his host, "You've won so many tournaments, Bob, you must know the right thing to say when they give you the trophy.

How about lending me one of your speeches? I may just need it before the week is out."

Demaret played the first nine on opening day in a gentleman's 37. He three-putted the 2nd hole for a 6 and needed three putts again on No. 8 for a par 5. There was no warning of the fireworks to come, so there were precious few witnesses when James Demaret of Houston took apart the vaunted back nine of the Augusta National course in an exhibition of golf as close to perfect as the Masters has ever seen.

The show began when Demaret lined a number one iron up to within one yard of the flag on the 10th hole and rolled in the putt for his first birdie of the round. On No. 11 he rammed in a thirty-footer for a second bird. He overshot the green on No. 12, but saved himself by getting down in two for a par. He produced a birdie 4 on No. 13, by canning a twenty-five-footer after being short with his second shot. No. 14 saw a regulation par.

The 15th brought temporary trouble. Trying unsuccessfully to carry the moat with his second shot, Demaret found his ball buried in mud and water. Much later he described the situation with a smile. "Showing complete fearlessness, I removed my red-and-blue suede shoes, rolled my chartreuse slacks up to my knees, and stepped into two feet of water to make the shot. I used a wedge and hit well. The ball sailed out and came down on the green."

Once past that pitfall Demaret put his suede shoes back on, sank his birdie putt, and then another one like it for a deuce on No. 16. On 17 he pitched to within five feet and holed out for his sixth birdie of the nine. On the 18th green Demaret's twenty-five-foot bid for another birdie just missed. The Texan settled for an even 30 strokes, a 67 total. He had used only twelve putts on the nine holes. His comment later: "A fellow has to get the breaks. I had my share today."

Demaret's 30 eclipsed by one stroke the previous nine-hole mark set by Willie Macfarlane in the U.S. Open of 1925. It equaled the record made by Francis Ouimet in the U.S. Amateur at Baltimore. But this April day in Georgia was to be so big a day for Texans that before sundown even Demaret's feat was pushed into the second paragraph of the overnight stories.

Shattering every existing record for a major tournament on a man-sized course, Lloyd Mangrum, the twenty-five-year-old added starter from Dallas, played his first round in 64 strokes. With 32-32, eight strokes under par, Mangrum equaled the best score ever made (by Jones in a practice round) on the National course. His mark still stands as a Masters standard.

The story of Mangrum's magnificent round is best told by a hole-by-hole description, which follows, with the distances as they were then:

No. 1, 400 yards, par 4. Drive and number five iron to thirty feet, two putts for a par.

No. 2, 525 yards, par 5. Drive and brassie to within forty feet, two putts for a birdie 4.

No. 3, 350 yards, par 4. Drive and number seven iron to six feet, one putt for a birdie 3.

No. 4, 190 yards, par 3. Number two iron to thirty-five feet, two putts for a par.

No. 5, 440 yards, par 4. Drive and number four iron to forty feet, two putts for a par.

No. 6, 185 yards, par 3. Number six iron to twenty feet, two putts for a par.

No. 7, 370 yards, par 4. Drive and number nine iron to fifteen feet, two putts for a par.

No. 8, 510 yards, par 5. Drive and spoon to fifteen feet, two putts for a birdie 4.

No. 9, 430 yards, par 4. Drive and number seven iron to fifteen feet, one putt for a birdie 3.

No. 10, 470 yards, par 4. Drive and number four wood to twenty-five feet, three putts for a bogey 5.

No. 11, 415 yards, par 4. Drive and number seven iron to twenty feet, two putts for a par.

No. 12, 155 yards, par 3. Number six iron to six feet, one putt for a birdie 2.

No. 13, 480 yards, par 5. Drive and number four wood to twenty feet, two putts for a birdie 4.

No. 14, 425 yards, par 4. Drive and number seven iron to fifteen feet, two putts for a par.

No. 15, 485 yards, par 5. Drive and brassie to forty feet, two putts for a birdie 4.

No. 16, 145 yards, par 3. Number seven iron to ten feet, two putts for a par.

No. 17, 400 yards, par 4. Drive and number eight iron to twenty-five feet, one putt for a birdie 3.

No. 18, 425 yards, par 4. Drive and number seven iron to thirty feet, one putt for a birdie 3.

Mangrum's card listed not a single eagle. He accumulated nine birdies, eight pars, and one bogey. He used thirty-two putts, and only on the last two greens did he score from farther away than fifteen feet. His forte was unwavering accuracy with his approach irons and woods. He never missed a green and hit five of them with wood shots.

Mangrum's 64 left him three strokes up on Demaret. Only two other players, both Texans, bettered 70 on the wind-swept course. Byron Nelson and Harry Cooper were tied for third place at 69.

After that remarkable day the 1940 Masters was something of a downhill glide, with Texas at the wheel. For the second round, in a move to make sure the heroics of Mangrum and Demaret did not become a habit, tournament officials cut the holes in the most difficult sections of the greens. At least one observer rated the course four strokes harder than the day before.

Mangrum came back to earth with a 75, still good enough to tie Demaret for the lead at 139. Nelson held third at 141. Amateur Bud Ward shot the day's best round, a 68. And Bob Jones, suffering from a painfully lame back, withdrew from competition after taking a 79-76.

At the end of three rounds Demaret had the lead to himself. His 70 was one better than Mangrum. Craig Wood, by now established as the nation's No. 1 runner-up, played himself into contention with a fine 31 on the front nine that included four straight birdies, starting at No. 2. He added another bird

Dwarfed by lofty pillars of pine Byron Nelson, winner in 1937 and 1942, tees off on the 11th hole, while Ben Hogan watches.

Threading a narrow path between water and spectators, Ben Hogan approaches the 16th green.

First Masters in 1934 featured Bob Jones playing his first
tournament in almost four years. Among sportswriters who
followed his comeback was Grantland Rice (wearing hat).
Jones tied for thirteenth place.

Ralph Guldahl tees off in 1937 tournament as his partner,
Bob Jones, watches. Guldahl finished second in 1937 and
1938, finally won the Masters in 1939.

Texas rivals Ben Hogan and Byron Nelson tee off in 1951. Nelson beat Hogan in 1942 play off. Hogan won in 1951, again in 1953.

Winning his first of three Masters in 1940, Jimmy Demaret prepares to putt on the final hole.

Champion again in 1947, Jimmy Demaret accepts winner's check from Bob Jones at presentation ceremony.

Surprise winner in 1946, Herman Keiser (*center*) is congratulated by Ben Hogan and Bob Jones. Hogan finished second after he three-putted the final hole.

Morgan Fitz, Augusta, Ga.

1948 champion Claude Harmon
(*right*) shakes hands with runner-
up Cary Middlecoff. Harmon's
279 tied early tournament record.

Morgan Fitz, Augusta, Ga.

A laughing Sam Snead gets his
first Masters jacket after winning
in 1949. Snead won again in 1952
and 1954.

at No. 7, and remained five under par through the 12th. But on the old devil 13th Wood got into the ditch and took a 6. He finished at 67, in a third-place tie with Sam Snead, three lengths behind Demaret.

A record crowd of ten thousand turned out for the final round. Fifteen hundred dollars and uncounted prestige hung on the outcome. But Demaret, who had complained of a stom-ach-ache the day before, went at his task with the aplomb of a Sunday golfer out to win a five-dollar Nassau. He strung together seventeen neat pars and a lone birdie (at No. 15). His 71-280 was enough for a comfortable four-stroke victory, the widest winning margin so far in the Masters.

The marauding Texans made a clean getaway with almost all of the five-thousand-dollar purse. Demaret took $1,500. Mangrum, despite a closing 74, finished second and earned $800. Nelson's third place was worth $600. Cooper tied for fourth at $400. Snead, in a seventh-place tie, got $200. And Hogan, right behind, settled for $100.

Jimmy Demaret's romance with the Masters had barely begun.

1941

THE onrush of the young Turks (or Texans) had to wait a year in 1941. The Masters had some unfinished business to complete—a legacy from the thirties. It involved a promise not yet fulfilled. And the suitor waiting persistently in the wings for his reward was the tall, blond, handsome New Yorker, Craig Wood, America's champion runner-up.

During the thirties Wood had more adventures than the hero of a dime novel, and more frustrations. A big hitter with his woods, Craig was billed by a manufacturer of golf balls as "the man who hits a brassie three hundred yards." But until he changed his style midway in his career, Wood was wild. "A hook kept me up to my ankles in crab grass for ten years and cost me a couple of major titles," said Craig.

As early as 1932 Wood led all money winners on the tour with seven thousand dollars. By early 1941 he had won sixteen tournaments of reasonable stature. But it was for losing—not for winning—that Craig Wood had become famous. He had lost in a play off or in the final match each of the three major championships of the day: the U.S. Open, the British Open, and the P.G.A. Twice he had the Masters championship swiped out of his hands.

Wood was a popular man. As he got older his frustrations played upon our national conscience, much as Princess Margaret's imminent spinsterhood bothered the British two decades later. Something had to be done, and the Masters was the natural vehicle.

Wood's career as a runner-up got properly started in the British Open at St. Andrews in 1933. He tied Denny Shute for the title. On the opening hole of their thirty-six-hole play off Wood hooked his second shot into a brook called Swilken Burn. Craig promptly took off his shoes and socks, waded in, and played his ball up to the edge of the green. But from there it took him three strokes to get down. Unnerved, Wood took another 6 on the 2nd hole and found himself a quick four strokes down to Shute. Six hours later Shute had won 149 to 154.

The next year Horton Smith's closing rush in the inaugural Masters left Wood in second place by one stroke. Later that summer Wood reached the finals of the P.G.A. only to lose to Paul Runyan. In 1935 it took Sarazen's double eagle to tie Wood in the Masters. When the play off was over Wood was runner-up again. In the 1936 Masters Wood suffered through a horrendous opening round of 88. He did a remarkable turnabout the next day with a 67, followed that with 69-76. But the 88 had left him beyond the help of any possible comeback, and someone remarked that Craig Wood's golf was like the little girl with the curl in the middle of her forehead.

For several years Wood had been bothered intermittently by a painfully sore back. The trouble probably could be traced to an automobile accident in 1932. When the pain struck it felt like a knife in the back. The injury was to dog Wood through his competitive life. In one 1936 tournament he stooped to pick his ball out of the 18th cup and couldn't straighten up. Wood spent a painful night in bed with a heating pad, but he stayed in the tournament and won it.

Like so many champions before and since, Wood went through a period when his game seemed to come apart at the seams. In 1938 he started turning in tournament scores in the 80's and was rarely even in contention. He failed to qualify for the starting field in the U.S. Open, and it was only by vote of his fellow pros that he was invited to the Masters of 1939.

At about this time Craig took the post as club professional at Winged Foot in Mamaroneck, New York. He laid off the tournament circuit for a while. When he did come back, early in 1939, he seemed to have a new spirit, as well as a putter that reacted to his commands like a well-bred field dog responding to its master.

But there was more frustration ahead. The 1939 U.S. Open at Philadelphia is remembered best for the fact that Sam Snead, apparently a sure winner, took an 8 on the final hole. Snead's blowup gave Craig Wood another crack at his first major title. He needed a final birdie 4 to tie Byron Nelson and Denny Shute for the title. To get it he hit what he has called the greatest shot of his career: a 260-yard brassie to the narrow green. He missed a fifteen-foot eagle putt that would have won for him, but he got his birdie and a tie.

In the three-way play off the next day Shute fell by the wayside early, and after seventeen holes Wood led Nelson by a stroke. But on the 18th Craig hooked his second shot and hit a spectator on the side of the head. State troopers carried off the unconscious man, and Wood, shaken up, missed a winning eight-foot putt. Nelson sank his putt for a birdie 4 and another tie. The next day Nelson won the second play off 70-73, and Wood's reputation as a runner-up remained unblemished.

By April, 1941, Wood was pushing forty and time was running out for him, as it was for many men that prewar spring. The ruling triumvirate—Nelson, Snead, and Hogan—were favored to win the eighth renewal of the Masters.

On opening day Craig Wood played the National course in 66 strokes. Wood's day started inauspiciously enough when he got mixed up in the trees on his first tee shot. But a seven-iron recovery put him close enough to the hole for a birdie 3. That was the spark that started him off on a great round, and when the field had finished for the day Wood was five strokes in front.

Rain and wind swept the course for the second round. Jug McSpaden played the first nine in 31, but settled for a 67. Nelson had a 69, and Wood had trouble. But Craig's putter saved him. He sank his first putt on each of the final four holes. That salvaged a 71-137 and three strokes of his lead over Nelson.

On the third day Hogan and Dudley played themselves out of contention with 75's. Snead had done the same thing a day before. McSpaden fell back. Nelson skidded to 39 on the front nine, and had to work for a 73-213. Sam Byrd, the reformed ball player who once had been Babe Ruth's understudy at Yankee Stadium, made his run with a 68. When Wood turned in another 71 he led Byrd by three strokes and Nelson by five.

The key shot of Wood's round was a spoon that he slapped across the ravine on No. 13. It set up a birdie 4, where most of his rivals had 5's and 6's, and one—Ben Hogan—had a 7.

Wood had been taking disappointments so long and so gamely that he had the gallery of eight thousand pulling for him as they had rarely pulled for a golfer before. He had a margin to work with: three shots over Byrd and five over the dangerous Nelson. This could be the day.

But after nine holes, Wood's lead was gone. He had used up 38 strokes, while Nelson, the brilliant Lord Byron, had turned in 33. It looked like the champion runner-up would keep that title after all.

But Wood, playing ahead of Nelson and puffing cigarettes at twice his usual smoke-a-hole pace, tightened his belt and refused to blow up. One hole decided the tournament. As usual it was No. 13.

Wood reached 13 first. His second shot just cleared the ravine and stopped on the apron. From there he chipped downhill four feet past the cup, then made his putt good for a birdie 4. Behind him came Nelson. Four years earlier Byron had caught and passed Guldahl on No. 13 with an eagle 3 in the wake of Guldahl's bogey 6. This time Nelson reached the wicked dog-leg one stroke behind, having taken a 4 on short No. 12. His drive was well to the right. His second shot, a long wood, was dead on the pin all the way. If it had legs to clear the ditch it would leave him putting for another eagle, which in all likelihood would win the tournament. But the ball landed short. It fell into the ravine in front of the green, and Nelson had to pick it out and drop for a penalty. He didn't even get his 5. His chip shot was too strong and left him with a good-sized putt. He gunned for it, and the ball hit the cup but refused to stay in.

Nelson still had a bare chance, but by now it hinged on Wood's making some mistakes. He didn't. With birdies on Nos. 15 and 16 he slammed the door in Nelson's face. Wood's 72, his highest score of the tournament, put him in at 280— three strokes better than Nelson, despite Byron's final round of 70.

The Masters had finally transformed its original bridesmaid into a bride. And Wood didn't let his case rest there. Two months later, wearing a tight corset-belt to ease the pain in his newly reinjured back (sprained while shaving two weeks before the tournament), Wood won the National Open at Fort Worth by a clear three-stroke margin.

At thirty-nine he became the oldest man so far to win the Open, and the first ever to win the Masters and the Open in the same year. After waiting so long Wood was able to wear his Open mantle a long time. Pearl Harbor made the national championship a wartime casualty, and Wood ruled as duration champ until 1946. His Masters reign was not so long. Augusta hosted one more April clambake and crowned one more champion before giving way to the war.

1942

THE gallery fidgeted on the apron surrounding the 18th green. They strained to see through fading light. Any stroke now could be the last, and no one wanted to miss it.

Gaunt Byron Nelson, the popular choice in this medal play off, knelt to size up his eighteen-foot putt. As he straightened up there seemed hardly enough weight on him to stretch over the six-foot, two-inch frame. At the edge of the green a sober-faced Ben Hogan crossed one leg in front of the other and leaned on his wooden-shafted putter. Hogan, the spunky little challenger, watched intently as Nelson stroked his putt. The ball covered the distance and disappeared into the cup. It was a winning par 4. The crowd reacted noisily, and Nelson's face broke into its familiar wide smile, as he legged it across the green to shake the hand of his victim.

Friends and fellow workers clamored around to congratulate the two golfers, as they stepped up to the committee table to receive their prizes: for Nelson, the winner, a new mid-iron fresh from the pro shop itself; for the runner-up, Hogan, a mashie, also new. Then everybody—contestants, gallery, and officials—went inside to celebrate the Glen Garden Golf Club caddies' Christmas party of 1927.

John Byron Nelson, Jr., was a fifteen-year-old caddy when he faced William Benjamin Hogan in that first dramatic play off for the caddy championship of Glen Garden. Young Byron had been born on a ranch in Ellis County, Texas, forty miles southeast of Fort Worth. His father, who was in the feed business, had moved the family to the city in 1922 when Byron was ten. In his early teens Nelson learned to golf by working at Glen Garden. He was a popular favorite with members and caddies alike.

Hogan, six months younger than Nelson, was born eighty-one miles west of Fort Worth in Dublin, Texas. His father, a blacksmith and mechanic, died when Ben was nine, and Mrs. Hogan moved her three kids to the city.

Ben was eleven and not very big, when he decided to earn some money (sixty-five cents a round plus tips) as a week-end caddy. Once in the caddy yard Ben discovered he would have to fight for his right to stay there. He did. And when enough older, bigger caddies learned the hard way that Ben Hogan never backed away from a fight, the kid from Dublin started to earn his first money in golf. Pretty soon he was golfing himself. A natural left-hander, Ben turned himself into a right-hander to fit the only clubs available.

In the 1927 match with Nelson, Hogan was the darkhorse. The play was to be nine holes, medal. The two boys played evenly for eight holes. Hogan parred the 9th for a 39. Nelson, lying 3 on the green, sank a thirty-footer to tie the match.

Hogan won the first extra hole 4 strokes to 6, but the match wasn't over. The men running the tournament decided the play off should go a full nine holes. So when Nelson sank his eighteen-footer on the 18th green he won the play off by a single stroke, 41-42. The defeat rankled young Hogan. The following year Glen Garden recognized Nelson by giving him a junior membership and the playing rights that went with it. Hogan, meanwhile, drifted off to municipal courses to play, and for many years he would not even visit Glen Garden. Things always seemed to come a little harder for Ben Hogan.

The world had spun upside down by the time Hogan and Nelson arrived in Augusta for the 1942 Masters. Hogan had turned professional in 1930, just before his eighteenth birthday. Nelson, after a period in which he had to sell his amateur prizes to make ends meet, turned professional at twenty in 1932. "Then I really starved," he recalled. Both young men had survived a long, heart-breaking stretch of poverty and failure on the circuit. Now both were on top.

Success had come first to Nelson. With his Masters victory in 1937 and U.S. Open title in 1939, he was the reigning champion of the game.

Hogan was going through a period when all he could win was money. He had dominated the earnings list in 1940 and '41. Again, in 1942, he was ahead of Nelson and Sam Snead, his closest rivals, in both money won and Ryder Cup points. But Ben could not win a major tournament.

Nelson, Hogan, and Snead were leading a parade of talented and exciting young players who had brought golf to a new high level of public interest. Each of the three was a household name already, and each left his fans with the distinct premonition that bigger and better things lay just around the next dog-leg.

Never particularly close friends, Ben and Byron had met head-on at least three more times since their caddy match in 1927. In 1940 the two played off a tie for the Texas Open at San Antonio. Nelson won by a stroke. They met again in the P.G.A. quarter finals of 1941, and Nelson was the winner by 2 and 1. Hogan got a measure of revenge in '41 by defeating Nelson 1 up in an intramural version of the Ryder Cup matches.

The United States had been at war four months as the Masters convened in April, 1942. When only forty-two of the eighty-eight invited players were able to show up the tournament had the smallest field in its nine-year history. In the gallery and around town uniforms outnumbered civvies by two to one. Near-by Camp Gordon had burgeoned as headquarters for the Fourth Motorized Division, U.S. Army. The Augusta National Club, using its own men and funds, was building a large driving range and putting green at the camp. Jones dedicated it on the eve of the Masters, saying, "I think this is a bigger contribution than money." He added that proceeds from the Masters would be used to equip and maintain the range for the soldiers.

P.G.A. President Ed Dudley announced that Franklin D. Roosevelt had given golf and other sports a green light to go ahead despite the war. The P.G.A.'s 2,300 members responded by pledging to raise $250,000 in 1942 for war relief.

Wagering men made Hogan, at 5 to 1, a slight favorite over Nelson, Snead, and Craig Wood, the defending champion. A poll of the pros favored Nelson, and Byron responded with practice rounds of 68, 71, 71. But Hogan, Jones, Sarazen, Sam Byrd, and Jimmy Hines were also warming up under par.

A clubhouse argument started over whether Sam Snead—billed in those days as the "hillbilly slugger"—might not play just as well or better in his bare feet. Sam obliged by removing his shoes and playing the first hole with a knot of reporters in his wake. He put an iron shot three feet from the pin for a birdie. At the 9th, barefoot again, he shot a par 4. Said Sam, "Maybe I ought to play this way all the time. That's the way I learned back home, and it feels better. Those shoes keep you too far away from the ground. Your toes can't grip in as well."

Old Guardsman Gene Sarazen kept the discussion going by remarking indignantly that Snead's performance was undignified and not worthy of the Masters, even in a practice round. If Sam persisted in going barefoot, warned Gene, he would play in kilts.

On April 9 Horton Smith and Paul Runyan shot 67's to take the first-round Masters lead. Nelson and Byrd had 68's. Jimmy Demaret came in at 70. Hogan took 73, and Bob Jones with a 72 matched par for only the second time in a Masters round.

Snead, wearing shoes but suffering considerable pain from a sore back, shot a 78 and said he might not be able to continue. Sarazen took an 80 and said he might join Snead on the sidelines. Nelson played the most consistent golf of the day, hitting fourteen greens.

Next day Nelson bagged a 67, and his 135 total for thirty-six holes cut two strokes off the record Craig Wood had set just a year before. But when Byrd turned in his second 68, Nelson possessed no more than a one-stroke lead. Runyan, Smith, and Demaret were tied at 140. Hogan's 70 put him at 143, eight strokes behind Nelson. Jones's 75 dropped him into a fifteenth place tie with Snead. Sore back, shoes, and all, Sam had snapped back with a 69. But it came too late to help him.

Nelson was superb again from tee to green, and only a mischievous putter kept him from opening a greater margin. Repeatedly his first putts nibbled at the hole, but the only one of consequence that dropped was a ten-footer for a deuce on No. 16. Thirty-four of his 67 strokes were putts. Gambling at No. 13, Nelson got home with a three-wood into the teeth of a stiff headwind for his birdie.

On the third day a boisterous wind swept the course, and Ben Hogan made his move with a 67. Nelson's putter was colder than ever. When three of his putts on the back nine went into the cup and popped out again Byron was glad to get home in even par. Sam Byrd, paired with Nelson, was obviously bothered by the company of almost the entire gallery. He took a double bogey 6 on the first hole and soon fell out of contention with a 75. Likewise Smith, Demaret, and Runyan fell back.

Only Hogan advanced. Unhampered by the wind he racked up six birdies, missed par only at No. 14 where his second shot went over the green. His card showed just twenty-eight putts, and the eight-stroke gap between him and Nelson melted to three.

Hogan kept coming on the fourth day. Nelson, still missing

most of his putts, struggled to hold on. With two holes to play Nelson still led by two. But on the 17th he cut his approach shot too fine and landed short in a bunker. When he missed a twelve-foot putt for par one stroke was gone. At the 18th Hogan dropped his approach a scant yard from the cup and rolled it in for a birdie 3. His total was 70-280. On the same hole Nelson missed another winning twelve-footer and took his par for 73 and a tie. So the second play off in Masters history was arranged: eighteen holes of medal play between the two best golfers in the world.

The Hogan-Nelson play off was a memorable affair—memorable for the golf troupers and P.G.A. officials, who made up much of the Monday gallery. Jones and Cliff Roberts were the official scorekeepers (their scribbled card is still on file at Augusta). As Roberts remembers, "Hardly a man who had played in the tournament left town. Everyone stayed over to watch the play. I don't believe any day of golf ever had more attention from golf people themselves."

Nelson slept very little Sunday night. A nervous stomach was giving him trouble, and he felt no better the next morning. The crowd sensed it on the first tee, when Nelson hit probably the worst tee shot of his life. The ball sailed toward a concession stand far to the right of the fairway, hit a pine tree, and lodged under a small fir. The ball was so close to the trunk that Nelson had to chip out left-handed. His third shot went over the green, and by the time he tapped down in 6 he was two strokes behind Hogan's regulation 4. Some of the less ambitious reporters present lost interest in the apparently one-sided match and returned to the clubhouse.

Both men birdied the long 2nd hole and matched par 4's on No. 3. Nelson lost an opportunity to gain on the 3rd green, when he missed a five-foot putt. On the short 4th Nelson bunkered his tee shot, and took a 4 to Hogan's par 3. Hogan led by three strokes.

Ben showed his first sign of weakness at No. 5, when he left himself a sixty-foot run-up from the edge of the green. But he got down safely in two for a par that left his lead intact. On

66

the 6th hole—185 yards, par 3—Hogan slipped, and Nelson started his move. Ben pulled his tee shot and it kicked off the green to the left. He chipped four feet over the cup and missed coming back for a 4. Nelson planted his tee shot eight feet from the pin and sank it for a deuce. Now Hogan led by one.

A missed seven-footer cost Nelson a chance to tie at No. 7. Hogan had to chip up from in front of the green, and he sank his putt for a halving par 4. The rugged 8th, 510 yards uphill, was Nelson's hole. He rammed a full spoon six feet from the flag and made his putt good for an eagle 3. Hogan hooked his second shot, had to pitch over a mound to get on, missed a short putt, and settled for par. Byron took the lead by a stroke. The Nelson stomach must have felt better.

Now Nelson was playing with cruel accuracy, almost knocking the pins out of their cups, and it was Hogan's turn to scramble. When both parred the 9th Nelson's card read 35, Hogan's 36.

The big 10th hole, perhaps the toughest par 4 in America, cost Hogan another stroke. He missed the left-hand fringe of the green with his second shot, chipped six feet long, and missed the putt. Nelson failed with a ten-foot birdie putt, but got his par. He led by two. Both men scored irreproachable birdie 3's on No. 11, Hogan sinking from twenty feet and Nelson, responding to the pressure, hitting from nine feet.

Nelson's tee shot almost hit the flag on 12. His ball stopped two feet away for a simple deuce. Trying to match it, Hogan's shot just failed to stay up. The ball rolled part way down the bank that separates the 12th green from Rae's Creek. From there he did well to earn his par, sinking a seven-footer to do it. Nelson stood three up. But now it was Hogan's turn to fight back.

Hogan drove short on the curving 13th, but his determined second wood carried the ravine. It carried over the green, in fact, but Ben lobbed back to within two feet for a scrambling birdie. Nelson reached the green in two and halved the hole. Again on 14 Ben banged out a birdie. When Nelson merely parred, his lead was cut to two. Hogan made it three straight birds on the 15th, chipping up from the left-hand side. Nelson three-putted for a par 5, and Hogan trailed by a single stroke.

But Hogan's comeback stalled on 16, when his tee shot over the water fell into a bunker. Nelson executed another perfect tee iron that left him four feet from a deuce. He missed, but picked up a key stroke anyway when Hogan needed three to get down from the bunker.

So the previous day's situation was repeated. Nelson stood two up with two to play. This time the outcome was different. Nelson had the easier par on 17. Hogan had to chip back and one-putt for his. With a two-stroke margin Nelson played it safe on the 18th by keeping his drive far away from the towering trees on the right. Hogan, cutting it desperately thin, caromed his drive off a tree and needed a spoon for his second shot. Both approaches landed in the sand, and both recoveries left ten-foot putts. Hogan gamely canned his for a par 4. Nelson, conceding a stroke, holed out carefully in two putts for the 5 he needed to win. The card read Nelson 69, Hogan 70.

So the Masters crowned its second double winner. Nelson had played eight holes, from 6 through 13, in six under par. Hogan played the same eight holes in even par, but lost six strokes to his opponent.

Nelson's final putt was the last shot fired in anger at Augusta for the duration. Three Aprils came and passed before the masters were able to gather again in 1946. Meanwhile, the course lay fallow, a grazing ground for club-owned livestock. Hogan and Smith could be found at O.C.S. Guldahl became a captain. Lloyd Mangrum and many others went overseas. Craig Wood tried to enlist but his bad back excluded him. Sam Snead became a sailor.

Byron Nelson was declared 4-F, because he suffered from hemophilia. He stayed home, and became this country's outstanding athlete of the war years. He helped raise many thousands of dollars for war relief; in both 1944 and 1945 the Associated Press voted him athlete of the year. In '45 he won nineteen of thirty-one tournaments, including thirteen in a row. The competition wasn't always what it might have been, but Nelson's fabulous stroke average—68.33 for 120 rounds—would have been hard to beat in any competition.

No more Masters titles were to fall to Nelson. By late 1946 he had a stomachful of competitive golf. He stashed his clubs in a corner and retired to a cattle ranch near Roanoke, Texas. But every year in April those clubs come out of hiding for the Masters, and almost every year Nelson, as though playing from memory, rises to the occasion, and the gallery sees flashes of the peerless player who caught Guldahl on one memorable day and beat Hogan on another.

1946

THE masters returned to Augusta in the first week of April, 1946. Fifty-one amateurs and professionals gathered to give the National course its first test in four years. They found it as beautiful and as treacherous as ever. They also found the winner's end of the purse up $1,000, to $2,500. The war had been over for eight months and the troops were back. The troops in this case being the likes of Hogan, Snead, Lloyd Mangrum, Demaret, Chick Harbert, Chandler Harper, Runyan, and Jones himself, who had started as a captain in the Air Force. Byron Nelson, the duration champion, was present, along with some others like Jug McSpaden and Sam Byrd, who had kept tournament golf alive through the war years. The old champs —Craig Wood, Horton Smith, Ralph Guldahl, and Henry Picard—were ready for another gallant fling. Among the newcomers were two young amateurs of promise: Frank Stranahan of Toledo and Cary Middlecoff of Memphis.

The wartime lapse had brought some new names to the fore. It had also cost some aging players their last precious years of

70

greatness. But for the two leading players of the decade, Ben Hogan and Byron Nelson, it was as though there had been no break at all. Ben and Byron renewed their rivalry of 1942 without missing a stroke. The golf buffs adapted a line from a movie advertisement of the day: "Hogan's back and Nelson's got him." In 1945 Nelson had won $66,000 and had swept the boards, except for an occasional challenge from Jug McSpaden, Sam Byrd, and Bob Hamilton. On the day the war ended there were those who said, "The party's over for Lord Byron. Now the rest of the big boys will be back." The competition did get rougher, but Nelson beat the best of it. He proved it doesn't matter who the competition is as long as you keep shooting birdies.

Only Hogan was Nelson's match. The two Texans kept up a cross-country duel for preëminence that lasted until Nelson retired late in 1946. Their rivalry got professional golf off to a running start toward a postwar boom.

Coming into the Masters, Hogan had the edge. He led the winter circuit in earnings with $12,000 to $7,600 for Nelson in second place. Nelson left the tour two weeks early to get ready to defend his title. In an exhibition in Atlanta Hogan whipped Nelson with a 66. Two days later the same pair got together for a little game in Augusta, and Nelson fired a 65 at Hogan. Their best ball total was 60.

On the eve of the tournament O. B. Keeler, the venerable and respected golf writer from Atlanta, listed his choices to win. Hogan and Nelson were on top, followed by Snead, Demaret, McSpaden, Byrd, Mangrum, and Lawson Little. Keeler's ninth choice was Herman Keiser.

Ninth place on anybody's list was perhaps a little high for Keiser, although he himself said he hoped to finish as high as sixth or seventh. Herman was a Navy veteran with big sad eyes, a long face, and longer limbs. He had won only one tournament of note, the 1942 Miami International Four-ball, in partnership with Chandler Harper. He was currently running ninth in the dollar derby with $3,576, most of it representing a second place in the Phoenix Open and another second in the

Greater Greensboro Open. He had tied for first place at Phoenix, but Hogan whipped him in a play off.

Keiser had come up by the classic route. As a thirteen-year-old schoolboy he started caddying in Springfield, Missouri, in 1928. On weekends he would rise at 3 A.M. and pedal his bicycle five miles, to be the first to register at the caddy shack. He came into his first full set of clubs by winning a caddy tournament at age sixteen, and in 1934 he won sixteen straight amateur tournaments. A couple of years later he turned professional on the strength of a second-place finish in the Louisville Open. Then he set up a driving range back home in Springfield and managed to win the Iowa State Open in 1938. Two years later he signed on as assistant pro at Portage Country Club in Akron, Ohio, where he soon established a course record of 60. The next year he became head pro at the neighboring Firestone Club, and set off for the first time on the winter circuit of 1942.

Along the way young Herman fortunately had crossed paths with two fine instructors. At Hickory Hills in Springfield he served as caddy master under Horton Smith, who had putted his way to two Masters championships, and putting—especially the long approach putt—became the strongest part of Keiser's game. In 1937 Herman came in contact with Henry Picard, who spent as much time helping struggling young pros develop their game as he did perfecting his own. Picard took Keiser's game apart. He told Herman to stand up straighter, address the ball farther back, lengthen his swing by taking a longer grip on the shaft, and revise his grip to bring the left hand under the right hand on top. "It will be a year before you get used to the new style and your game improves," warned Picard. He was right.

Keiser cut short his fling at the circuit in 1942 to enlist in the Navy. He spent thirty-one months as a storekeeper on the cruiser *Cincinnati*. One day in Bangor, Ireland, Keiser, on liberty from the *Cincinnati*, played the first seventeen holes of the local course in 63 strokes. "You're a cinch to break the course record," his partner told him, and they walked toward the final tee. But Herman never found that last tee. The 18th hole at Bangor had been converted into a Victory Garden.

Keiser spent his final summer in the Navy operating the base driving range in Norfolk, Virginia. Paul Runyan and Chandler Harper were with him, and the three sailors spent their free time reviving their games and looking forward to the day when they could set off again on the tournament tour. When his discharge finally came Keiser went back to his job at Firestone, where he promptly won the Seiberling Open. Then he headed west to follow the sun.

The Keiser biography is presented here in answer to the question that rang through an incredulous gallery and was echoed across the country on the evening of April 4, 1946: "Who the hell is Herman Keiser?"

Keiser had fired a 69 in the first round of the Masters to share the lead with another, better-known ex-G.I., Chick Harbert of Detroit. Almost no one saw him do it. As fitted his stature at the time Keiser was a member of a group known as the Dawn Patrol or the Dew-Sweepers Brigade. These are the unknown players, who get the early morning starting times in every tournament. They are off and playing before the big-name pros have finished their breakfasts and before most of the galleryites are out of bed. Keiser was in the third twosome to tee off this particular morning, but it is doubtful he would have attracted much of a crowd even if he had gone off at high noon. The quiet Missourian was a slow player, with a shuffling gait and an orthodox up-and-down swing. He was built for distance—6 foot 1, 180 pounds—but he was not a slugger off the tee, averaging perhaps 230 yards. "I know it's no fun to watch me play," said Herman. "In fact, it's painful."

Blustering winds and the guile of two old-timers combined to give the gold-plated field a rough opening day. George Sargent, National Open champion in 1909, and Dave Ogilvie were out at dawn finding tricky places to sink the pins. As a result, only five players were able to break par. But the slippery greens and well-placed pins were no hazard for Keiser. He shot four birdies on the first six holes and finished with a 69 that included just twenty-six putts.

Chick Harbert played with a rare prewar ball given to him just before he teed off. He earned his 69 by scoring four 3's on the first five holes and finishing up with birdie putts on the 16th and 17th. Vic Ghezzi, Tony Penna, and Fred Haas, Jr., were tied at 71, two strokes behind the leaders.

Where were the favorites? Byron Nelson had managed a 72. Hogan had 73; Snead 74; and Jones, Demaret, and Byrd had 75. The bell tolled for four former champs. Smith, Wood, Picard, and Guldahl ranged from 78 to 85. Never before had a darkhorse won the tournament or even come close, so Keiser's early position was not taken seriously.

On the second day the headlines went to the old master, Jones. Listening to advice from Walter Hagen to "take your time at the top of your swing, get lazy again . . .," Jones played the front nine in 34 and seemed ready to move into the thick of the fight. As *Time* magazine described it, "The Old Master [Jones] teed up against Byron Nelson, 34, the modern mechanical marvel. Most of the way, Jones matched Nelson shot for shot. Bobby's haymaker swing, accentuated wrist motion, and hula hip motion seemed incurably individualistic beside Byron's three-quarters swing, and minimum of motion. . . .

"Next day, Bobby edged Byron one stroke with a 72—his best competitive round in a dozen years."

Jones's 72 left him in fourteenth place at 147. More ominous to the pros was a 68 by one Herman Keiser. At 137, Keiser was five strokes up on Jimmy Thomson, who was in second place. Harbert fell out of the lead with a 75. Hogan lay seven behind Keiser at 144. Nelson had 145.

"Keiser took only twenty-six putts again," noted Hogan, "and I think thirty-one putts is championship caliber."

"Keiser will win," predicted Nelson. "He is too sound a swinger and too good a putter to give up a five-stroke lead."

After fifty-four holes Keiser still led by five strokes, but now it was Hogan who occupied second place. Keiser had scrambled home in 71, his third straight round under par. He had stood

74

two over par after fourteen holes and seemed to be buckling. But the 15th hole saved him. He chose his favorite club, the three wood, for his second shot; the ball barely cleared the water hazard and stopped on the front apron. From there he chipped in for an eagle 3. He also rolled home a ten-footer for a bird on No. 17.

Hogan started his famed finishing kick with a third-round 69, despite a 6 on the 13th hole. Ben was no better than par after fourteen holes, but he birdied three of the last four holes and served notice.

In 1946 and for a dozen years thereafter the closing drive of Ben Hogan was a thing of menace on the golf course, more dangerous than lightning or downhill putts. To have Hogan, with his steely gaze, his immense powers of concentration, and his flawless shots closing in on you was like running from the bogeyman in a nightmare. The experience aged boys into men and men into old men. The established players usually faced up to the challenge with something of a fatalistic air. The young and less sturdy usually folded up completely—usually, but not always.

Herman Keiser teed off for his final round, with Hogan thirty minutes behind him in hot pursuit. Nelson and the others had failed to make a move, so the championship lay between the thirty-three-year-old Hogan and the thirty-one-year-old Keiser. One had brought top price in the pre-tournament Calcutta auction, while the other had been sold in the "field" like a broken-down claimer.

Keiser had led the tournament for three days. After the second day he began to realize he had a chance to win. Now he knew he was the only man standing between Hogan and Ben's first Masters title. It was an unenviable position. Playing erratically, Keiser parred just two holes on the first nine. But he managed a 37 on the strength of three scrambling birdies. Hogan made the turn in 35 and closed the gap from five strokes to three.

Playing it safe when he could and scrambling when he couldn't, Keiser parred the next eight holes. On short No. 12

he had to chip on and one-putt. On 15 his third shot was headed over the green until it hit a lady spectator and bounced back. He got his par.

Meanwhile, Hogan had been putting in hard luck, just missing the cup time and again. But on the 12th he finally dropped a fifteen-footer for his deuce. On the 13th he reached the extreme left edge of the green in two. The cup lay twenty-five feet away at the bottom of a steep slope. On that lightning-fast green it seemed impossible for him to stop the ball anywhere near the hole. But Hogan trickled his approach putt down the hill to within a yard of the cup. His birdie 4 brought him up to within a stroke of Keiser. Ben three-putted the next hole, but he got that stroke back with a birdie on the 15th.

At that moment Keiser was playing the 18th. His second, a magnificent shot from the rough, struck the flagpole and bounced twenty-five feet to the right and above the cup. Herman went bravely for the birdie he felt he needed as insurance against Hogan, but his sloping putt ran five feet beyond the cup. He missed again coming back. That meant a three-putt bogey 5 and a 74-282. "I've lost it," muttered Keiser, and he turned to the clubhouse.

Hogan needed three pars to tie, a lone birdie to win. He parred 16 and 17, his putt on the latter grazing the side of the hole. Two good shots to the 18th green left him with a twelve-foot putt to win. Keiser waited in the clubhouse and prayed against a tie. "Let him win it or lose it now," said Herman, "but don't put me in another play off with Hogan."

Hogan stroked his first putt and turned away. "The moment I hit it I knew it was going to miss the hole," he said later. "So I turned my head for a moment. When I looked back I saw the ball had passed the hole and I was amazed to see it hadn't stopped within a foot of the cup."

The ball had come to rest thirty inches below the hole. Hogan putted again for his tie, and the ball slid just past the side of the cup. Hogan, like Keiser, had a bogey 5. Ben had made up five strokes to catch his man, then chucked it all away by three-putting the final green from twelve feet.

76

Exclaimed Herman Keiser, the winner by a stroke, "I'll be back here every year if I have to walk fifteen hundred miles to do it."

Said Ben Hogan, "It just wasn't my time to win. But there's another year coming."

1947

WHEN heard from last James Newton Demaret, the people's choice, was heading home to Houston with the 1940 Masters championship tucked in his well-tailored pocket. The excited citizens at home threw a banquet in James's honor for the third time that winter. They rechristened a boulevard in his name, and according to legend seriously considered naming a brand of Scotch after him.

"I took it for granted I would follow in my father's footsteps," Jimmy told them. "He was a painter and carpenter. But I started playing golf when I was twelve, and I soon learned that I could follow through with a brassie better than I could with a paintbrush or a hammer."

Demaret could also follow a day's golf with an adventurous night on the town. He was the life of the party wherever he went, with a flair for the good life unseen since Walter Hagen in his prime. Jimmy further endeared himself to his friends by faithfully picking up the check.

Whether it was a reaction to the night life or merely a streak of bad luck, Demaret's game turned sour that summer of 1940. His putts wouldn't drop. In the U.S. Open at Canterbury he took eighty-one strokes on the first round and didn't even bother to turn in his card. For Demaret the year might as well have ended in April on the final green at Augusta.

But in 1941 Jimmy got back down to business. He took a club professional's job at Wee Burn in Darien, Connecticut, and went into serious training. For six weeks he played twenty-seven holes a day, in a campaign to perfect his putting on the Eastern greens. The tonic worked, and before long the Demaret golf game was again in a class with the Demaret personality.

By 1947 Jimmy was permanently established among the leaders of golfing society. He was thirty-five, an age which in those days was considered on the shady side of the bunker. But Jimmy actually seemed to be improving with age. There was so much else to notice about Demaret, however, that people rarely considered his game. Take his wardrobe, for instance. He admitted to owning seventy pairs of slacks, twenty jerseys, fifty-five shirts, and eighteen sports coats. The sartorial stir he created made him the darling of the sports clothes manufacturers. His wife complained that when they traveled together there was barely room in their luggage for a couple of dresses for her.

On one trip to England for the Ryder Cup matches Demaret astounded the British by appearing on the first tee in a pastel green pullover, crushed strawberry trousers, and an emerald green silk knitted cap. On succeeding days he wore pillbox red with a cerise cap, and heliotrope with a daffodil yellow cap. The effect was almost too much for Britain's postwar austerity program.

Demaret was paired in a twosome with Byron Nelson in the first round of the 1947 Masters. For Nelson, this was the first tournament appearance in six months. He had retired to his Texas ranch late in 1946 and announced that henceforth he would play only in the Masters. "I found myself playing more golf at 3 A.M. than at 3 P.M.," said Nelson, "so I threw my clubs in a corner and didn't even look at them until about a week ago."

If anyone hoped Nelson had come to Augusta just to shake hands with old friends they were quickly disillusioned. A friend of Byron's, possibly as a joke, offered to give him a prize bull for his ranch if he could break 70 on the first round. That was all the extra incentive the retired champion needed, and he spun around the National course in 69 strokes. On No. 13 two perfect shots left him fifteen feet from the cup and he canned the putt for an eagle 3. Nelson's performance inspired Demaret, who also subtracted three strokes from par with three birdies and fifteen pars to tie Byron for the lead.

Seven players were bunched at 70, a stroke behind Nelson and Demaret. The tournament favorite, Ben Hogan, was not one of them. Ben had lost four strokes to par between the 9th and 14th holes and finished with 75. Bob Jones was another at 75. Herman Keiser, the defender, was at 74. So was Bobby Locke, the South African champion, who was playing his first competitive round in the United States. Dr. Cary Middlecoff, who had just turned professional, was one of the six tied at 71. Sam Snead was even par 72.

Demaret still shared the lead after thirty-six holes, but this time his co-leader was young Middlecoff. Carey fired a 69, Demaret a 71; and the two were bracketed at 140. Nelson's 72 put him a stroke behind, in a tie with Jim Ferrier of Australia and Tony Penna. Hogan had the best round of the day, a 68, and Jug McSpaden registered 69. But both lagged three strokes behind.

By the third evening Demaret finally had the lead to himself. Third-round jitters attacked both the leaders, but while Middlecoff soared out of contention with a 76 Demaret scrambled masterfully for a 70. Errant drives kept Jimmy in the tall Georgia pines most of the morning, but his chipping and putting saved him. On six of the first seven holes he got down in one putt, after missing the green on his approach. Altogether he one-putted ten greens, and William D. Richardson of the

New York *Times* observed that "fate had its finger on this man."

Three strokes behind were the Gold Dust Twins of the wartime era, Nelson and McSpaden. Hogan trailed by four.

For his final round on Easter Sunday Demaret appeared in a stunning new spring ensemble of canary yellow. "If you're going to be in the limelight you might as well dress for it," said Jimmy. Demaret dressed up to his reputation and played up to it as well. He executed his fourth straight sub-par round —a 71. Amateur Frank Stranahan shot a 68, to come within two strokes of Demaret's 281 total, and finished second. Nelson and Hogan could do no better than 70, and McSpaden shot 71.

So James Demaret, who enjoys being on a golf course, won again on the course he enjoys the most. He joined Nelson and Horton Smith on the plateau reserved for two-time winners of the Masters. This time he went on from Augusta to make 1947 his finest year. He led the field in earnings with $24,000, and his low scoring average won him the Vardon Cup.

1948

ALL winter thirty-one-year-old Claude Harmon patiently taught rich men how to play golf at Chris Dunphy's swank Seminole Club in Palm Beach. Around the first of April he began to think above moving his wife and their three youngsters up to Mamaroneck, New York, to begin his summertime job as head pro at Winged Foot. But first Claude Harmon wanted a vacation. So he stopped off at Augusta to swap a few tall stories and play golf.

Claude had never won a major tournament in his life and he had no illusions about this one: the 1948 Masters. He had played here the year before, but had finished far down the list. He had qualified for another invitation only by coming in twentieth in the U.S. Open. Besides, Claude knew there was some truth in all that has been written and said about the club professional. The teaching pro is the backbone of the game, the unsung hero who stays at home and tries to cure Waldo Sneedbee's hook and Mrs. McFungo's slice, while all the glamour boys are off chasing rainbows and pots of gold on the tournament tour.

Of course, there were arguments in favor of the life of the home pro. Claude knew them too, from stops at Northmoor in Chicago, Winged Foot (as assistant to Craig Wood he ran the shop while Craig was away winning the 1941 Masters and U.S. Open), River Oaks in Houston, Lochmoor in Detroit, and finally back to Winged Foot in 1946 to succeed Wood, his best friend. Harmon was on his way to becoming one of the great teachers of the game. His crop of "chicks"—Winged Foot assistants, who eventually left the coop and climbed to bigger things —was to include a succession of fine golfers: Jack Burke, Mike Souchak, Dick Mayer, Dave Marr, Al Mengert, Harry Dee, Shelley Mayfield, Otto Greiner, and others.

But in April, 1948, Claude Harmon was fully aware of one simple truth: The teaching pro may occasionally get sprung long enough to play in the big tournaments, but he never wins one.

You don't just walk in and steal the prize from the likes of Hogan, Nelson, Snead, Jones, Mangrum, Middlecoff, Demaret, Locke, Ed Furgol, Harbert, and Sarazen. All of these were in Augusta, and more. So, stocky, convivial Claude Harmon came along more or less for the ride.

On opening day Lloyd Mangrum posted a 69, and his boss at Chicago's Tam O'Shanter, George S. May, offered him a thousand-dollar bonus if he won the tournament. Harmon shot a comfortable 70, as did his friend Ben Hogan. Hogan was off to his finest year so far, but he still hadn't won his first major championship.

On the second round Harry Todd of Dallas produced a hot 67 and took the lead at 139. Harmon shot another 70 and slipped into second place. On the 15th hole his second shot had lodged in the grass just short of the green and just above the water line. Claude calmly shed his shoes and socks, waded into the water, and pitched his ball to the green for an eventual par 5.

The next day Harmon strolled blithely along, while so-called "tournament tough" players cracked up all around him. On No. 11 he hit a three-iron shot three feet from the flag and got his first birdie. On No. 12 he earned a deuce with a putt of six feet. He went for the green on 13 with a four iron, got home safely, and was down in two putts for another birdie. Claude turned in a card of 69, and found himself two strokes up on the field after fifty-four holes. Hogan with 77, Mangrum with 75, and Todd with 80 all fell from contention.

Harmon came out for his last round before a record crowd of eleven thousand fans. He had been born in Savannah, and most of the gallery was rooting for the first native son of Georgia to win the tournament. Claude, who had played his early rounds almost in solitude, reacted to the pressure by becoming taciturn. The only man with a good chance to catch him was hard-luck Chick Harbert, famous for his tremendous drives and sad finishes. Harbert started the day just two strokes off the pace, but he fell apart and finished with a 76.

Harmon, a little more on edge himself now, showed the strain by biting his lips and asking the crowd about his drive: "Where is it? Where is it? Did anyone see my ball?"

He sweated for pars on the early holes and lost a stroke on No. 4. But on the short 6th his tee shot hit to the right of the pin, kicked left in a wide arc, and ran straight for the hole. It dribbled to a stop six inches short. The rattle of applause from the gallery brought a faint smile from Harmon as he tapped in his first birdie. "That was the big shot," he said later. "I don't mind telling you I was nervous till then. But that did it. Something clicked."

At the 7th he holed a twelve-footer for a birdie 3. A perfect spoon shot up the hill on No. 8 left him six feet from the cup, and he holed out for an eagle 3. Harmon had played Nos. 6, 7, and 8 in four under par, and the verdict was as good as his.

There were still some anxious moments on the back nine. His tee shot on the 12th fell short at the edge of the creek, and his pitch from there went almost to the 13th tee. But he salvaged a bogey 4. On No. 13 Harmon's bold second shot fell into the shallow edge of the creek; he waded once more into the

84

water (this time with his shoes on) and splashed it out and onto the green for a par 5.

That was the final obstacle. Harmon finished with another 70. His 279 total tied Ralph Guldahl's tournament record, set in 1939. His five-stroke margin over Cary Middlecoff in second place broke all records.

Claude picked up a check for $2,500 and headed north for Winged Foot. His vacation was over.

1949

FOR six years, beginning in 1949, the story of the Masters and the story of golf itself hangs on two men: Ben Hogan and Sam Snead. Both men had been near the top of their profession for a decade. Hogan, the self-made champion, was a hundred-forty-pound "iceman," whose palms were one solid callus from hitting more golf balls than anybody else who ever lived. Snead was a strapping natural athlete with the perfect swing, who feared no living man but "yipped" over three-foot putts. Both men were approaching their thirty-seventh birthdays when 1949 began, an age at which most earlier golf champions had either retired or slipped quietly down the hill. But this was a new era in which champions worked harder, lasted longer, and got richer. For half-a-dozen years Hogan and Snead were to dominate the game completely, unrivaled except by each other. For another half-dozen years the magic of their names kept them first in the public mind, long after they had stopped winning the big championships.

Between them Hogan and Snead won five of the six Masters

George Schaeffer, Augusta, Ga.

Heroes' bench near 18th green holds eight former champions *(from left):* Byron Nelson, Jimmy Demaret, Sam Snead, Gene Sarazen, Claude Harmon, Herman Keiser, Horton Smith, and Henry Picard.

Presidential foursome at Augusta National brought together Byron Nelson, Dwight Eisenhower, Ben Hogan, and Clifford Roberts, tournament chairman.

Losing gamble is reflected on the face of Billy Joe Patton in 1954, as his second shot on No. 13 goes into a ditch. Patton finished hole with a 7 and lost his lead.

Leading finishers in 1954 were Billy Joe Patton (290), Ben Hogan (289), Host Bob Jones, and Sam Snead (289). Snead defeated Hogan in play off.

Morgan Fitz, Augusta, Ga.

Surrounded by thousands of fans Arnold Palmer adds up his score after winning the Masters Golf Tournament of 1960.

The Masters Club dinner in 1960 brought present and past champions together *(seated from left):* Horton Smith, Gene Sarazen, Jimmy Demaret, Sam Snead, Bob Jones, Art Wall, Clifford Roberts, Claude Harmon, Doug Ford, Arnold Palmer; *(standing)* Jack Burke, Henry Picard, Craig Wood, Cary Middlecoff, Byron Nelson, Herman Keiser, Ben Hogan. Ralph Guldahl is missing.

A Sunday gallery forms a zigzag pattern, as it spills
over the rolling fairways of the Augusta National.

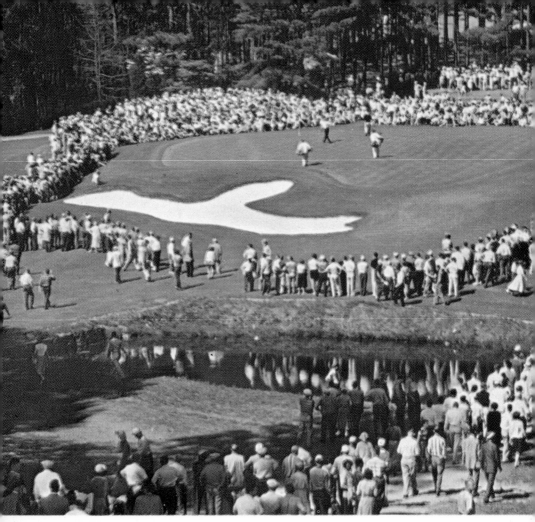

Encircling a green, the gallery makes use of every vantage point on what is undoubtedly the finest spectator's course in golf.

tournaments from 1949 to 1954. Only Jimmy Demaret, in 1950, was able to break through the Hogan-Snead axis.

Hogan had established himself as the nation's leading player in 1948. He won the U.S. Open at Los Angeles with a record 276, then added the P.G.A. and the Western Open, to become the first man to win those three championships in a single year. As usual he was golf's top official money winner with $32,000, and his average of 69.3 strokes per round earned him the Vardon Cup. Ben started out equally well in 1949, earning $3,800 in his first four tournaments. But by Masters time Hogan was in bed at home, recovering from a fractured pelvis, broken collarbone, and fractured rib. In February he had narrowly missed being killed when his car collided head-on with a bus on a lonely Texas highway.

So the first turn fell to Sam Snead.

In 1937 when Snead asked his new bosses at the Greenbrier in White Sulphur Springs for time off to play in his first Masters, they let him go. But they docked him one week's pay: ten dollars. Sam finished 18th in that first try. In eight succeeding tries it was thirty-first, second, seventh, sixth, seventh, seventh again, twenty-second, and sixteenth. He qualified for the bridesmaid's club in 1939, when he finished with a record 280 only to have Ralph Guldahl play the final nine in 33 and beat him.

But Sam's hard luck at the Masters was insignificant, compared with his frustrations in the U.S. Open. His 8 on the seventy-second hole in the 1939 Open was the first and most memorable reversal. In 1947, on the final green at St. Louis, he missed a putt of 30½ inches. Lew Worsham, who had asked that both putts be measured, then sank one of 29½ inches to beat him.

Legions of fans loved Snead as much for his weaknesses as for his great talent. Perfection alone is not much fun to watch. But if Snead was anything, he was human. The cash customers shoved and stretched to watch Sam's awesome, pasture-bred swing and booming drives. Then they stampeded to the green, secretly hoping for a glimpse of the great man as he blew a two-foot putt. Sam regularly gave them what they expected on both counts. But in 1949 he fooled them.

He arrived in Augusta with a new putter. It was a sixteen-ounce club with a T-shaped brass head, true-tempered steel shaft, and a cork grip. Fred Matzie, a Los Angeles clubmaker, had made the putter for Stanley Kertes, the pro at Bryn Mawr Country Club in Chicago. It bore the trade name "Velvet Touch". As Kertes told it, "I was using the club on the putting green one day just before the Los Angeles Open, when Snead came along and asked if he could try it. It was the weight of the head that he liked the most on that first try. I said I'd let him have it after the Tucson Open in early February—about a month later. It's a lucky putter, all right. I gave it to him at Tucson, and he went on to win five of his next seven tournaments with it."

Snead also changed his style of putting. With his old mallet-head putter he would roll his wrists. "I discovered," said Sam, "that you can't possibly roll your wrists forward exactly the same way you roll them back, so you can never be accurate that way." With the new putter Sam kept his wrists stiff.

Snead sailed into Augusta on the crest of two victories in two weeks at Aiken and Greensboro. In prize money he was running second only to Lloyd Mangrum. On opening day a strong wind lashed the course, and only six of the fifty-eight contestants managed to break par. The best of these was Mangrum, the mustached Texan, whose 69 strokes included one shot from out of a bunker on No. 7 that rolled into the cup. This was the third time that Mangrum had led on the first day. Snead required a 73 and was tied for eighth place.

The wind blew again on the second day and Snead, to the dismay of his gallery, rose two strokes higher to 75. In a normal year his 148 might have put him out of contention. But Mangrum slipped to a 74-143; and Herman Keiser, the 1946 winner whom everyone had forgotten by now, putted his way to a 68 and a share of Mangrum's lead. Snead, instead of being out of it, lay only five strokes back.

The winds were gone by the third morning, and a hot

Georgia sun beat down on the big Saturday crowd. At this point Snead and his gift putter went to work and stole the show. After parring the first hole Sam reached the par five 2nd green in two and got his birdie. At the 4th hole he dropped a deuce putt from twenty-two feet. He followed this with an eight-footer for a bird at the 5th, and when he sank a fourteen-footer on the 9th for his fourth birdie Sam was out in 32.

Walter Hagen had once told Snead, "It's all in your mind, Sam. You're the only man in the world who doesn't think you're a good putter." Perhaps now Snead's mind was changing. He three-putted the 10th as the gallery groaned, but he birdied 13 and again on 15, where his eagle putt bounced in and out of the cup. Three pars brought him home in 67. At 215 he was one stroke behind Johnny Palmer, the former B-29 gunner, who had fired a 70 to take over the lead. Mangrum, with a 72, now shared second place with Snead.

Herman Keiser had run into a little trouble on the 2nd hole. His drive strayed into the trees. From there his second shot rolled into a creek, and he dropped out with a penalty. He needed two more to reach the green, then he three-putted for an 8. That finished Herman.

Johnny Palmer shot a respectable 72 for his final round, and Mangrum had a good 70. But they were no match for Snead. A throng of fifteen thousand waited for Sam at the first tee, and he set out to give them a lesson in power *and* putting they would never forget. At No. 1 he dropped a twenty-footer for his 3. At No. 2 he used an iron to reach the 535-yard green in two and birdied again. He settled for par on No. 3, but at the short 4th he rolled home a fifteen-footer for his deuce. Bogey and two pars followed. But at the 8th he birdied from ten feet away, and at No. 9 he saved his par with a seven-footer. Snead was out in 33 and burning up the course.

Sam suffered bogeys on Nos. 10 and 11, but at 12 he rammed his putt home from ten feet for another deuce. He added birdies at 13 and 15, and saved one final thrill for the throng that surrounded the 18th green. Snead's drive on the home hole faded into the woods on the right, but he had room to swing his club and sent a mighty seven iron shot to the green. From eighteen feet he sank the last putt for a birdie 3 and another 67, to win by three strokes. He had used just thirty putts. Snead picked up his ball, looked at the adoring gallery, and asked in his best mountain drawl, "Who started that story about I can't putt?"

Ben Hogan was not the only regular missing from the 1949 Masters. Bob Jones, convalescing from an operation on his back, failed to start for the first time. Jones watched the play through field glasses from the porch of his cottage near the 10th tee, and on the final day he used an automobile to follow Snead on his spectacular round.

1950

A FRUSTRATED golfer once muttered, "The guy who designed that 13th hole at Augusta, they ought to hang him to a tree." Bob Jones might laugh and point out that this nature-made hole required no designing at all.

No. 13 (named the Azalea hole for the bright pink and red bushes that blossom among the pines) runs along the southern boundary of the National course, far enough from the main channels of traffic so that thousands in the gallery never see it at all. It is the kind of hole the average player relishes: a sporty par 5, short enough, at 475 yards, not to require great power, with hazards of wood and water that are interesting but not discouraging. Three decent shots practically guarantee the average golfer his par, and a good approach gives him a fighting chance for a bird. But No. 13 is not that simple. Coming where it does, midway in the final nine, on the heels of two demanding par 4's and a delicate par 3, No. 13 is the key hole of the Masters—the kingmaker. A dozen times or more the capricious 13th has withheld its favors from one candidate, and bestowed them, without rhyme or reason, on the eventual winner. Such was the case in 1950. The Masters that year had much that commanded attention: Ben Hogan's courageous return to competition, Sam Snead's ailing back, Jimmy Demaret's outrageous clothes, and Jim Ferrier's superlative putting. But in the end, No. 13 stole the show.

Hogan was back, and for the first time in his life he was a sentimental favorite. In January, eleven months after his accident, he had returned to tournament golf in the Los Angeles Open at Riviera. He had chosen his spot carefully. Caddies called the Riviera course "Hogan's Alley." Twice he had won the Los Angeles Open there and once the U.S. Open. As the world watched, Hogan tied for first place this time. But the play off was one trip too many for Ben. He lost by four strokes to Snead, who had replaced him as the number-one man in golf.

At Augusta the giant galleries that had followed Snead in 1949 switched to Hogan, hoping that the gritty little man would at last win the one big title that had eluded him. Ben had the old lean and hungry look and he insisted, "I never felt better." But he wore rubber stockings for support and soaked his legs in a hot bath between rounds to relieve the ache. Hogan began his bid with a 73 that included three putts for a par on No. 13.

Snead, who had added the P.G.A. title, the Vardon Cup, and top money-winning honors to his 1949 Masters victory, opened his defense with a 71. Sam was operating with a sore back, the same maverick vertebrae that had bothered him off and on since boyhood, and which he predicted would one day end his golf altogether.

Jimmy Demaret appeared in chartreuse trousers, a sweater of stunning salmon pink, and green suede shoes. His opening 70 included a birdie 4 on the 13th. Also at 70 was Jim Ferrier who went around in just 27 putts.

Skee Riegel, a former U.S. Amateur champion from Tulsa, held the first-day lead with a 69. But Riegel took a 75 the second day and was not heard from again. Hogan aroused the crowd with a string of four birdies, beginning at No. 6, that put him out in 32. Ben had trouble only at the 13th, where his second shot dropped into the water and he took a six. A second round 68 gave him second place at 141.

Jim Ferrier took over the halfway lead with a 67-137. A strapping two-hundred-pounder, Ferrier had a trick left knee —the result of an injury incurred while playing football in his native Australia. Favoring the knee put a dip in Ferrier's backswing. But it didn't bother his chipping and putting, as he sank six birdie putts.

Back in the pack, Snead slipped to 74 when he strayed into the water on No. 13 for a 6. Demaret was a sight to behold in white knitted shirt with red piping around the form-fitting sleeves and neckline, lavender slacks, and lavender shoes trimmed in pink. One look at Jimmy demanded a second, because at first glance the pink trimming on the shoes appeared to be his bare toes breaking through. Demaret's golf was ragged, but a masterful eagle 3 at No. 13 earned him a 72.

Ferrier's putter kept him in front on the third day. He used just 29 strokes on the greens, as he put together a 73. Of his 210 strokes for fifty-four holes, only ninety were putts. Hogan set out relentlessly to catch Ferrier, and as he climbed wearily up heartbreak hill to the 18th green he needed but one more birdie to tie for the lead. Ben had a downhill putt of twenty feet, much like the one he had needed to beat Keiser four years before. He tapped the ball lightly, but it rolled three feet past the cup. Coming back, Hogan missed again. A 71 left him two strokes behind Ferrier, with the final eighteen to play.

Snead was five strokes off the pace after a 70, and Demaret trailed by four. Once again Jimmy's golf was less startling than his appearance. He sauntered forth in trousers of old rose, with a neatly matching rose-and-white shirt. The shirt featured a high neckline, circling gracefully above a dickey. His game featured another eagle 3 at 13, which saved him another par 72.

For the fourth round on Easter Sunday, after an appreciative glance at Jimmy, most of the crowd followed Hogan. But this was not Ben's day. His bid had expired on the 18th green the afternoon before. Sunday he went out in 38, and when he caught the creek again on the 13th, for a 6, he was through. A 76 tied him for fourth place at 288. Snead slipped into third position with 72-287.

Demaret went out in 35, birdied the 13th, and turned in a 69 for 283. Pretty sure of second place he sat back and waited for Ferrier.

The big Aussie was two under par for twelve holes, when word of Demaret's finish reached him. A casual 38 on the last nine was all he needed to win. But first he had to get past No. 13. Ferrier's drive on this hole hooked into the brook on the left. He dropped out two clubs lengths from the hazard for a one-stroke penalty. Cautiously he played his third shot short of the ditch. But his next shot bounced well past the pin, and he took two putts for a 6. On the scoreboard Ferrier was still ahead. But his harrowing experience on the Azalea hole had beaten him. The trusty putter that had rifled home one prodigious putt of sixty feet on the front nine now deserted him. He could get only one par on the final six holes and finished with a ruinous 41-75, two strokes above Demaret.

In winning, Demaret had played the 13th hole four times in 4-3-3-4, six strokes under par. He played the other sixty-eight holes in one over par. In contrast Ferrier had used up nineteen strokes at No. 13, Snead twenty, and Hogan twenty-one.

As the first three-time winner of the Masters Demaret added a houndstooth jacket of chartreuse and brown to his playing costume. He stepped up to the microphone on the putting green, and after accepting congratulations all around sang a song which he dedicated to himself: "Do You Know How Lucky You Are?"

1951

GOOD things had always come slow and hard for Ben Hogan. As a boy he was a natural left-hander and had to train himself to use right-handed clubs—the only ones available. When the caddies got together for their casual games little Ben tagged along, swinging awkwardly. When a brilliant group of teen-age amateurs, including Byron Nelson and Ralph Guldahl, was burning up Texas courses with scores of 70 and below Ben was struggling to break 80. In his unrewarding early years on the circuit people wondered how long Hogan could stay with it and why he bothered to stay at all. Even Ben's first U.S. Open championship in 1948 came late. Nelson, his caddy-yard contemporary, had won *his* first Open nine years before. Then in 1949, with the golf world finally at his feet, came Hogan's accident, and the little man had to start climbing all over again.

Hogan's comeback reached an early peak in June, 1950, when he won the U.S. Open at Merion in a dramatic play off with George Fazio and Lloyd Mangrum. Now only the Masters eluded him. Nine times in thirteen years he had tried for this one. His misses included a 1942 play off loss to Nelson and a three-putt final green loss to Keiser in 1946.

Hogan trained his sights on the Masters of 1951. He still wasn't strong enough to stand the weekly tournament grind. At the Phoenix Open, in fact, he had to withdraw because of illness. But he played in the Seminole Four-ball, then headed for Augusta almost two weeks earlier than anyone else. For ten days he haunted the practice tee and studied the National course as it had never been studied before. Hogan planned his tournament tactics: a safe, medium drive on No. 1; a punched four iron instead of the orthodox five iron on No. 16; when to gamble and when not to on No. 13; always to play safely to the right on No. 11, where the water hazard had recently been widened to encircle the left side of the green.

When the tournament began Hogan was still running his caddy to a frazzle on the practice tee. After the first eighteen holes George Fazio led with a 68. Snead had 69 and Hogan 70. Said Ben, "I was more pleased with how I played than how I scored."

After round two Skee Riegel owned the lead at 141. Hogan was second at 142, Snead third at 143. Ben admitted, "I couldn't be playing better."

With one round to go Snead and Riegel shared the lead at 211. Hogan hovered one stroke back after a 70. Said Ben, "Snead is the man to beat. The leaders usually fade, but I can't depend on that. I've got to let go."

The next day Ben let go on the front nine. With a gallery of eight thousand trailing him he clipped off birdies at two of the first three holes, was out in 33, and took over the lead. Riegel was in early with a 71-282. Snead had met disaster at the remodeled 11th hole. His long approach shot caromed off the right-hand slope, ran over the putting green and into the water on the left. Sam hit again and splashed once more. He finally took an 8 after reaching the green in 6, and shambled home with an 80.

Now Hogan switched to the defense to protect his lead.

96

On No. 10 he two-putted cautiously from six feet. On No. 11 he stayed far to the right, chipped on with a six iron, and got his par. Approaching the 13th green he pulled a four iron from his bag, then exchanged it for a six iron and played short. His third shot was a short pitch over the ditch, and he sank a seven-foot putt for a birdie. Again at No. 15 he played short of the water, and settled for a par.

Two more pars left him needing only a bogey 5 on No. 18 to win. This time Hogan's tactics left no room for long down-hill putts. He deliberately played his second shot thirty yards short of the green. From there he pitched his third up to within four feet and rolled in the putt that sealed a 68. A faultless round of fourteen pars and four birdies brought him in at 280, two ahead of Riegel.

After Bob Jones had helped Ben into his first Kelly green Masters jacket a reporter asked Hogan what tournament he would like to win next. Said Ben, "If I never win another one, I'll be satisfied. I've had my full share of golfing luck."

1952

ON THE face of it the Masters of 1952 appeared to be a wide-open free-for-all. Prize money had been increased to twenty thousand dollars. Record galleries, which reached sixteen thousand on the final day, were heavily dotted with Korean War uniforms from nearby Camp Gordon. Among the six-dozen entrants were all the famous names of golf. But as things turned out the tournament became an old-fashioned two-man fight between a pair of old Masters, Ben Hogan and Sam Snead.

For three hard days Hogan and Snead beat off the challenges of sharp newcomers like Tommy Bolt, a Durham, North Carolina, driving range operator; Jackie Burke, the sensation of the winter tour, and Dow Finsterwald, an Ohio University undergraduate. By the final round the customers had forgotten the rest of the field. They split into two massive galleries and squinted through cardboard periscopes to watch the two old antagonists.

Hogan had added the U.S. Open to his 1951 Masters victory.

Snead came in as reigning P.G.A. champion. On opening day both men carded a 70, each doing it in his own distinctive style. Hogan, playing with silent precision, took one bogey, thirteen pars, and three birdies for his best first round effort ever. Snead, brilliant but more erratic, would have been lower except for two tactical errors. On the first hole he overplayed the green and took a 6. On the 13th his drive fell into the brook. He struck a rock on his first attempt to recover and took another 6.

Snead was nearly perfect the second day. He birdied the first two holes, added three more birds at 12, 13, and at 15, where he played a six iron to the green from a rutted roadway. A 67 put him three strokes up on Hogan and the field. Sam, not forgetting the Hogan hex, was optimistic nevertheless.

"I'm riding a hunch that's almost infallible," he said. "Almost every time I play the short holes in par or better, I win. Right now I'm three under par on the little ones. I've had four deuces, three three's and a four."

Some of the bounce went out of Snead on the third round. It was a sunny, cool day, but a wild thirty-mile wind sent scores soaring. Hogan, first out of the two, missed four greens on the front nine and turned in 39. But on the second half he interspersed three birdies on the first six holes and managed to get home in 74. Snead took 4's on the first two holes, and for a brief moment he stood five strokes up on Hogan. But after that Sam could do little right, and a discouraging 77 left him deadlocked with Hogan at 214.

Now it was Hogan's turn to make a prediction. With classic brevity he discussed his chances through a tight-lipped smile: "The low score will win."

Hogan may have been noncommittal, but the experts were not. In any showdown between an unpredictable Snead and a relentless, machinelike Hogan the odds had to be with Hogan. Snead teed off one hour before Hogan, wearing a pull-over sweater to match his familiar cocoanut straw hat. Sam played steadily through eleven holes. Then at the 12th, the hole Lloyd Mangrum once called "the meanest little hole in the world," came the slip most of the crowd had been waiting for. Strained by the knowledge that Hogan was stalking him from behind Snead slapped his tee shot into Rae's Creek. He dropped a new ball short of the creek, and the obstinate pellet landed in a depression. From there Sam's next shot was almost as bad as the first. It barely hung on the heavy grass embankment, just over the water and short of the green. Sam lay three and seemed a cinch for a 6 or more. But standing awkwardly with his left foot above the bank and his right deep in the grass, he executed a miraculous chip shot that bounced onto the green and rolled squarely into the cup. Snead had saved a 4, and the moment of potential blowup was over. He finished with a sturdy par 72 and 286.

Meanwhile, things were happening to Hogan that weren't supposed to happen to an "automatic" man. The skittery greens, trimmed to a nub, got the best of Ben. Five times he three-putted. Altogether he putted forty times on the eighteen holes. He finished with 79, seven strokes behind Snead, and at 293 no better than tied for seventh place in the final standings.

Snead, watching from the radio platform as Ben straggled up the last fairway, observed, "I guess Hogan is human after all."

The little man was quick to agree. He accepted his defeat with a stoic rationalization. "I've no complaint," said Hogan. "After all, I've lost more tournaments than I've won."

1953

THERE has never been a better golfer than Ben Hogan in 1953. The years of gritty determination, the interminable lonesome hours on the practice tee, where he hit more golf shots than any man who ever lived, now paid off in full for Hogan, as he approached his forty-first birthday. Between April and July he executed the "Professional Grand Slam," winning the Masters at Augusta, the U.S. Open at Oakmont, Pennsylvania, and the British Open at Carnoustie, Scotland. No other man, before or since, has accomplished this. He came as close as any professional player could come to matching Bob Jones's Grand Slam of 1930.

Nobody was surprised when Ben turned up in Augusta two weeks early for the Masters. Everybody figured he needed the practice. After losing the Masters to Snead and the U.S. Open to Julius Boros in 1952 Ben had retired from tournament play for ten months. It had been four years since his near-fatal accident in 1949, but Hogan still had to conserve his energy with all the care of a desert prospector nursing his last ounces of drinking water. He saved it for the big moments.

After eleven practice rounds Ben spent the day before the tournament just puttering around the putting green. He admitted, "I'm in grand shape."

A record field of seventy-three players had gathered. Lloyd Mangrum shot a practice round of 63, one stroke better than his competitive course record of 64, which was still unchallenged after thirteen years. Boros, the Open champion, shot a 67.

All the former winners except Guldahl and Keiser were on hand. A Masters club had been formed, and Snead, as defending champion, hosted a dinner for the membership. Most exclusive, the club included only the eleven men who had won the tournament, plus Jones and Cliff Roberts as honorary members. The National course was in nearly perfect shape, the fairways superbly conditioned, and the greens moderately fast. The newly inaugurated U.S. president, Dwight Eisenhower, had recently shot a 79 on it; and Hogan predicted the tournament record of 279, shared by Guldahl and Claude Harmon, was about to be broken. He neglected to say by whom.

On the first day Hogan shot a 70, good for third place behind Chick Harbert at 68 and Ed "Porky" Oliver at 69. The next day Hogan moved into the lead with a 69 for 139, and on the third day Ben ran away with the championship.

Porky Oliver, a jovial 220-pounder playing out of Palm Springs, California, was paired with Hogan for the third round, and he made a gallant bid to stop the runaway. Oliver started the day three strokes behind Hogan at 142. He shot a fine 67. But Hogan trumped that with a 66, his best Masters score, to give himself a four-stroke margin on Oliver and the field.

Marching side-by-side down the fairways, the big, garrulous Oliver and his gaunt little partner gave the gallery a performance to remember. Hogan was outweighed but not outdistanced off the tees. His second shots practically knocked the flags out of their holes. Oliver's putting was magnificent. On the 1st green he holed an eight-footer for a birdie. He sank an uphill fifteen-footer for another bird at the second. Hogan also birdied No. 2, and both men parred No. 3. They

102

matched deuces at the 4th. Oliver slipped to a bogey on No. 5, then parred the next four to be out in 34. Hogan held at par for three holes, then birdied the 8th, and topped off his nine with a prodigious birdie putt of sixty feet on the 9th green. He was out in 32.

Oliver started the second nine with a pair of 5's. Hogan putted twenty-five feet downhill for a birdie 3 at the 10th, and barely missed another on the 11th. They shared pars on No. 12, and both reached the 13th green in two—Hogan with a four wood and Oliver with a four iron. Ben three-putted for a par 5, and Porky gained two strokes by sinking an eagle from twenty-five feet.

Hogan compensated somewhat with an easy bird on 14, atfer his long approach stopped four feet from the cup. Both men birdied the 15th. At 16 Oliver gained two strokes again with a deuce, while Ben three-putted for his only bogey of the round. Hogan parred in on the last two holes for a 34-66. Oliver, in a last grand gesture, birdied the 18th for his 33-67. Between them, Hogan and Oliver had built a best ball score of 31-29-60.

But the competition was over. A rainstorm hit the course on the morning of the final round, but for Hogan and Oliver, starting late, the rain served only to slow down the greens to a reasonable speed. Oliver shot a 70 to tie the old record of 279. Hogan, plodding on legs that ached from the damp weather, shot a 69. His total was 274, five full strokes better than Oliver, the field, and the record.

Said Ben, "It was the best I have ever played for seventy-two holes." Then he added, "I hope I can come back next year and play the same caliber of golf."

"If you do," joshed his final-round partner, Byron Nelson, "you'll be playing here all by yourself."

For Sam Snead, defending champion, it had not been a happy week. Never in contention, Sam finished in a tie for sixteenth place at 292. Now the Masters score stood two for Hogan, two for Snead.

1954

IT HAS been said that the Masters is really two tournaments in one: the first is getting from the tee to the green; and the second, a separate struggle, is getting the ball into the cup on those big, undulating greens.

The Masters of 1954 was certainly two tournaments in one, but in quite a different way. The first, played over the regulation four days and seventy-two holes, belonged to an unknown amateur, who turned it into a personal, if not official, triumph.

The second was an historic play off between those two old pros, Snead and Hogan, who dueled head-to-head for a championship that turned out to be their last one at Augusta.

Tournament Chairman Cliff Roberts, going over the list of amateur players to be invited to the 1954 tournament, asked Bob Jones if the alternates to the Walker Cup team shouldn't be invited along with the regular team members. Jones agreed. He had played as an amateur himself and was anxious to see more of them compete in the Masters. Besides, no amateur had ever won the tournament, and only one, Frank Stranahan in 1947, had even come close.

So it happened that an invitation was dispatched to Morganton, North Carolina, for one William J. Patton, thirty-one, Wake Forest graduate, Navy veteran, lumber salesman, long-hitting but erratic week-end golfer, and alternate Walker Cup member for 1953.

Billy Joe Patton responded with alacrity. The boys at Mamosa Golf Club had been beating him regularly at two dollars a clip on their Saturday rounds. This would show them.

Billy Joe stepped up to the tee for his first shot in the driving contest the day before the tournament, crew cut and smiling, with the sun reflecting off his rimless glasses. He reared back and hit his drive with a swing that might have belonged to Babe Ruth. The ball traveled 338 yards. Patton had two more tries coming. "No thanks," said he. "The next shot I might miss altogether. I couldn't possibly beat that first one."

Nobody else could beat it either.

Thunder, lightning, and torrential rain caught part of the field out on the course on opening day. It was only the first installment of weather that was to produce the roughest playing conditions since the middle thirties and the highest scores in history.

Ben Hogan, grumbling about the difficult positioning of the pins, said, "Why don't they give each twosome a Seeing Eye dog to help them find the holes." But Hogan went around in a contending 72. Snead had 74. Billy Joe Patton, playing his first Masters round, shot a 70 to tie for the lead with Dutch Harrison.

The press sensed a story. Possibly a great upset was in the making, and at least here was a refreshing new personality: carefree, calm, and supremely quotable. They swarmed around Patton in the clubhouse.

"Now hold on a minute, boys," said Billy Joe. "Let's not go too strong on this thing. Tomorrow I may shoot an eighty."

The press was captivated, and the next day the galleries were, too. Patton kidded himself and the crowd through eighteen holes of woods and water for a 74. No one in the field equaled par, and Patton found himself where no amateur had been before: alone in the lead at 144. Hogan was a stroke back at 145 and Snead three behind at 147.

All along Billy Joe had been predicting his own blowup, and when it came early on the third round Patton was the least surprised of all. Billy Joe went three over par on the first seven holes, but he refused to crack completely. He birdied the 8th and 9th and managed to get around in 75. That tied him for third place at 219. Hogan and Snead, meanwhile, were resuming their accustomed places at the head of the class. Hogan shot a 69 for 214 and the lead. Snead, after a 70, trailed Hogan by three strokes.

It looked like another exclusive Hogan-Snead party. But Billy Joe Patton wasn't finished yet. His shenanigans in the fourth round gave the big boys fits. Several hundred excited North Carolinians converged on Augusta to swell the Patton gallery. Billy Joe played the first five holes in even par. On the 6th hole he chose a five iron and looked down the steep slope to the green 190 yards away. The pin was placed dangerously close to the edge of the green, and trouble. After changing his stance twice Patton dug in and hit. The ball cleared the front edge of the green and bounced toward the cup. It hit the pin a foot above the ground, spun down, and lodged between the pin and the side of the cup. The crowd gave a mighty shout that reached Snead and Hogan far across the course and did little for their peace of mind. Patton, after asking official advice from Joe Dey, executive director of the U.S.G.A., carefully removed the pin. The ball dropped to the bottom of the cup for an accredited ace. It was the sixth hole in one in Masters history, but the first ever scored by a man in position to win the title.

That shot gave Patton new confidence, and he started playing more boldly than ever. When he parred the 7th, birdied the 8th, and birdied again at No. 9 the crowd was sure it was following a winner. By going out in 32 strokes Patton had passed Snead, who needed 37, and tied Hogan, who later reached the turn in 37.

What happened next to Billy Joe Patton shouldn't happen to a fellow like Billy Joe Patton. But it did. The second nine at Augusta is designed for the bold player, to reward him when his gambling works and penalize him when it doesn't. Patton drawled, "I didn't come here to play it safe."

Billy Joe started the back stretch with three straight 4's, just missing his bird at No. 10 and chipping on for a bogey at No. 12. On No. 13 his drive was not very long, but he took a four wood and went for the green anyway. The shot was short and fell into the shallow creek. Patton slipped off his shoes and waded in after it. But when he saw his lie, Billy Joe decided not to try to play out. Instead he took a penalty stroke and dropped out. Still standing in his bare feet he pitched toward the green, but it was a weak effort and the ball did not reach the putting surface. He stopped to put on his shoes and socks, then he chipped short of the pin for his fifth stroke. Two putts gave him a 7. Double bogey.

The crowd moaned in disappointment. But Patton, walking to the 14th tee, turned to them and said, "C'mon, folks. Let's smile again." By the time all had reached the next green the smile was contagious, for Patton holed a birdie 3. But on the 15th Patton again tried to carry the hazard in two, and again he landed in the water. The result was a 6. From there, Patton, disappointed certainly but still good-humored, parred in for a 71-290. Simple par 5's on 13 and 15 would have given him 287.

Snead, meanwhile, had found his game. After being two over par for the first five holes he played the final thirteen holes in two under and finished with a 72-289. Hogan was playing about three holes behind Patton. When he reached the 11th hole he somehow had not been informed of Patton's 7 on the 13th. Hogan still thought he had to go all out for birdies to win. So pressure from an upstart amateur did something to Ben no professional opponent ever had been able to do. It forced him into a tactical error.

Because of the water that circles the left-hand side of the 11th green and the angled slope just to the right and short of it Hogan had made a rule always to approach safely to the right. He was content to chip on and one-putt for his par. But this time Ben aimed a three iron straight for the flag. He hooked it into the water and took a 6. Later he said, "If I'd known what happened to Patton I would have played it safe."

The 6 put Hogan three over par for the day. He played it close to the vest after that, staying even with par and finishing with a 75 that tied Snead. Their 289 was the highest score ever to head the Masters, and it set up an eighteen-hole medal play off for the next afternoon.

Billy Joe had lost by a stroke, but he didn't have to go home to face the boys in Morganton empty-handed. With him went a gold-and-silver cup for the best amateur score, a gold medal for best amateur score, a crystal vase for low score in the first round, a crystal cup for the hole in one, and a gold money clip for winning the driving contest. Regardless of what happened in the play off, 1954 would always be referred to as "Patton's year" at the Masters.

THE PLAY OFF

BEN," said one sun-tanned, middle-aged businessman to the other, "what would you say to splitting the pot, so neither of us has to walk all that way tomorrow for nothing?"

"What's the difference between first and second money, Sam?" was the reply.

"About fifteen hundred dollars, I guess."

"No thanks," came the answer.

Some fourteen thousand fans and an April sun turned out to watch the two titans in their Monday play off. On the first tee Hogan said, "Good luck, Sam." Snead replied in kind, and for the next three hours no more than a few phrases passed between the two men. Hogan walked silently, lighting each new cigarette with the butt of the last. Snead eased the tension by joking occasionally with the crowd. The evenness of the match was apparent from the start. At the 4th green Snead three-putted, and Hogan took a one-stroke lead. But Snead pulled abreast at the 6th by holing out from six feet for a deuce. They reached the turn in twin 35's.

At the 10th Snead's approach went over the green, but he chipped back sixty-five feet into the cup for a birdie and went ahead for the first time. At the 12th it was Hogan's turn to pull even, when Snead trapped his tee shot and took a bogey 4. Inevitably, No. 13 was the turning point. Hogan's cultivated fade had been breaking more than usual all day, and Snead had been outdriving him consistently. Sam's drive on the 13th carried twenty yards beyond Ben's. Hogan played a four iron safely short of the creek. But Snead gambled on a long two iron, and he carried the green. Hogan pitched to the front edge and needed two putts from there for a 5. Snead, twenty feet from the cup, came close on his first putt and tapped in the second for a 4 to take the lead.

Hogan went two down at No. 16 by muffing a three-foot putt, and he was still two down as they trudged up to the 18th green. Hogan was on in two, but Snead was trapped seventy-five feet away. Sam pitched from the trap to within five feet, and when Hogan's desperate birdie try from twenty feet out missed, Snead carefully used two putts to get down for a one-stroke victory, 70 to 71.

Said Hogan, "Sam played good golf, and I putted badly."

Said Snead, "I was a little luckier than Ben today. But then," he added thoughtfully, "I guess the sun don't shine on the same dog's tail every day."

Now the Masters score stood Snead 3, Hogan 2. And that's where it stands today.

1955

SAM SNEAD came out confident and grinning to defend his title in the Masters of 1955. He swept around the first nine holes in 34 and was still two under par when he reached No. 13, the hole where he had gone in front of Hogan in their play off a year before. Snead's drive on 13 was good, and he hit a second wood shot that cleared the dangerous ditch. But then one of those misadventures befell Snead that have plagued his career.

A new sand trap had been installed on No. 13 beyond the creek and just to the left of the green. Sam's ball found the new trap and buried itself in the sand. Snead stood on the turf outside the trap a foot or so above the ball and tried to blast out. His first attempt only drove the ball deeper into the sand. Now he lay three. On his next attempt he hit the ball flush on top with the blade of his wedge. It didn't move at all— four. Holding his temper, Snead remembered that a ball cut open the way his now was could legally be replaced without a penalty. Sam made the substitution, and on his next try the ball trickled down into the center of the trap. He finally came out in 6 and was down in two putts for an 8. It was a typical Snead experience, and Sam took it stoically. He played the remaining five holes in one under par. But instead of a 68 or 69 he turned in a card of 72.

The first round lead went to Jack Burke, Jr., a recent graduate of Claude Harmon's training school at Winged Foot. Burke, whose golfing father had finished second in the U.S. Open of 1920, shot a 67. Snead's 72 tied him for fourth place with a group that included Dr. Cary Middlecoff, the Memphis dentist. Hogan had 73.

Cary Middlecoff, an intense, high-strung but likable person, was capable of blistering hot streaks of golf. He was capable of cold streaks, too. Cary was 34. He had been golfing since the age of seven, when his father, a practicing dentist, had given him a cut-down set of clubs. Cary graduated from dental school in 1944, and went directly into the Army dental corps. "I pulled seven thousand teeth," he said later, "before I found out the Army had another dentist."

The Army experience was enough dentistry for Middlecoff, and when he got out he turned seriously to golf. His father asked Bob Jones to advise Cary against turning professional. Jones gave the advice, but Middlecoff ignored it. In 1947 he turned down a Walker Cup trip to become a pro. The next year he finished second (to Harmon) in the Masters, and in 1949 he won the U.S. Open. In the years that followed, Middlecoff's name was usually near the top, but those cold streaks—usually on the greens—made him wonder if he would ever win another important tournament.

Just before the 1955 Masters Cary remodeled his putter. It was the same club he had used in winning the Open six years before, but he built up the handle to the thickness of the grip on a driver. The new "feel" of the club, perhaps actual, perhaps mental, started helping him on the greens. On the second round at Augusta Middlecoff got hot. He opened with a birdie, followed it with four pars, and then went off on a burst of four consecutive birdies. That brought him to the turn in 31, a new course record. On the second nine Cary cooled off a few degrees as he started off with three comfortable pars. He reached the 13th hole five under par.

Middlecoff is perhaps the slowest and most fidgety of all golfers. He can rarely play a shot without working up to it with several tugs at the vizor of his cap, a brief exploration of the territory around him, a long look at his target, a hike of the trousers, a pause to dry his right hand on the seat of his pants, and another tug at the vizor—all the while frowning in dark concentration. It is a style that can drive players with him and behind him mad. But this same nerve-racking intensity communicates to his galleries, and the atmosphere becomes electric when Middlecoff is pouring it on. Six thousand people watched nervously as Middlecoff pushed his drive to the high right side of the 13th fairway. There was a hush as he went with his spoon on the second shot. The ball cleared the creek and rolled to the very back right edge of the green. The pin was placed at the front of the green, seventy-five feet away. Middlecoff paced the green. He inspected, sighted, scrutinized, and studied the line of his long, long putt. Finally he stroked the ball, and for seven long seconds the gallery held its breath as it rolled quickly across the center of the green, slowed down, then crept off a final slight break, and fell into the hole. Middlecoff stood transfixed, his fists clenched on the putter, as the crowd went wild. The sensational stroke was the longest important putt in memory. Bob Jones, watching from his motorized cart, called it "a delightful thing to see." The putt could not have been any longer, for there was no more room on that green and no broader green on the course.

Middlecoff floated home with a 65, seven strokes under par and one stroke short of the course record. Hogan had shot a 68 to take over second place, but he was four strokes above Middlecoff's 137. Hogan was still four strokes behind the next evening after Cary turned in a steady 72.

The final twenty-four hours were torture for the nervous dentist. He wasn't scheduled to tee off until 1:42 P.M. He

112

couldn't sleep. He bought the Sunday papers Saturday night and purposely saved them till Sunday morning. But by 9 A.M. he had finished them. He played Glenn Miller records on a phonograph until he was ready to throw the machine out the window, but it was still only 10 o'clock. He read old magazines until 11, then he bathed, shaved, and drove to the club for a big breakfast. He killed some time talking in the locker room, hit a few shots on the practice fairway, and finally it was 1:42. Hogan had teed off half an hour before.

Ben had started his pursuit coolly and methodically. From tee to green he was nearly perfect. Had his putts been dropping he would have been able to put considerable pressure on Middlecoff. But time after time Hogan's ball shunned the hole. He needed an eight-footer for his birdie on No. 2, a twelve-footer for a bird on No. 3, and another twelve-footer on the 4th. He missed them all. On No. 5 he three-putted from thirty-five feet. When he missed another short birdie putt on the 6th green Hogan's bid was over. Now the only man Middlecoff had to beat was Middlecoff.

Cary chattered nervously as he played, but he was hitting the ball hard and his putting was strong. His playing partner, Byron Nelson, returned the chatter and managed to keep the pressure at a minimum. Middlecoff completed the first nine in 34, but on the 10th hole he pushed his iron into a trap next to the green and took two getting out for a double bogey 6. He was still shaky on the 11th, but a good break saved him. On his approach shot to that dangerous green Middlecoff came up too quickly with his two iron. The ball never climbed more than three feet above the ground. But it stayed on line as it bounced down the slope, over the mounds, and onto the green. It was what duffers call a "good miss." Cary putted twice for his par, and his last attack of jitters was over. On the next hole he sank an eighteen-foot putt for a birdie 2.

As they walked to the 13th tee he asked Nelson, "I don't see what can happen now, do you?"

"No," answered Byron.

Nothing did happen. Middlecoff played the final holes

strong and safe. He played short of the water on both 13 and 15, and got his birdie on 15 anyway by pitching to within four feet of the cup. On the 18th he finished with a flourish, sending a six-iron three feet past the pin, and holing out for a birdie 3 and a 70. With 279 he was seven strokes better than Hogan for the widest margin any Masters winner has ever had.

As he slipped into his first green jacket Middlecoff offered some advice on how to play the National course. "I've finally learned that it's a waiting kind of course," said the deliberate dentist. "You'll get a chance for birdies if you wait for them. But if you shoot for birds, you'll bogey every hole."

1956

FORTY-TWO amateurs were invited to play in the twentieth Masters tournament. Among them was Ken Venturi of San Francisco. Venturi was a slender, dark-haired twenty-four-year-old, who had recently finished an overseas hitch with the U.S. infantry. The service interruption kept him from qualifying for a Masters invitation, although he had managed to beat Harvie Ward for the San Francisco city championship a month before. Instead, Venturi's bid to the 1956 tournament came from the past winners of the Masters, who each year vote to invite one "deserving player" not otherwise eligible.

Young Ken was the son of a professional, and, perhaps more important, he was the protégé of two important men of golf: Ed Lowery and Byron Nelson. Lowery, a member of the Augusta National club, was a San Francisco automobile dealer. Between rounds of golf Ken worked for Lowery selling cars. Through his boss Venturi had met Nelson in 1952. In their first round together Venturi shot a 66, but on the

18th green Nelson said to him, "Meet me here tomorrow at 9 A.M. There are six or seven things in your swing that need adjustment."

So the young amateur became the pupil of the two-time Masters champion. Ken went on to earn a place on the Walker Cup team in 1953. Like Nelson he became brilliantly accurate with his long irons. But the next January Venturi went into the Army, and when he came out late in 1955 something was wrong with his swing again. Lowery put in another call for Nelson.

"We got together at Palm Springs," recalled Venturi. "When Byron saw me swing he was so surprised he nearly fell out of his golf cart." Nelson went to work, curing the loop in Venturi's backswing and adjusting his stance to equalize the distribution of weight on his feet. Venturi recovered quickly, finished fifth in the Phoenix Open, and upset Ward at San Francisco.

On opening day at Augusta Venturi set the Masters on its ear with a 66. His playing partner was Billy Joe Patton. "Billy Joe kept telling me I could knock them in, and I did," said Venturi, who hit sixteen greens in par and sank his first putt eight times. The 66 was the lowest Masters round ever recorded by an amateur. But scores were generally low on that first day, thanks to a lack of wind and intermittent showers which slowed the greens. Cary Middlecoff, the defending champion, was only a stroke behind with 67. Tommy Bolt and Shelley Mayfield had 68's and Ben Hogan a 69. Five others players also broke par.

The greens were drier and faster on the second day, and a tricky wind that reached gusts of fifty miles an hour confused the players. Hogan faltered to a 78. Bolt and Mayfield had 74's. Middlecoff settled for par 72. Only two players broke par. One was Jack Burke, Jr., whose 71 hoisted him into seventh place at 143. The other was Ken Venturi.

On his second round Venturi proved he could scramble when he had to. His drives were crooked and his irons the same, but he retained a perfect touch around the greens. He bogeyed the second hole after being stymied by a tree on his drive. But he made up for that with a birdie on No. 3. After two strokes on the long 8th hole Venturi was still separated from the cup by 108 feet and two small hillocks. He chipped sharply with a six iron, and the ball bounced onto the green and into the cup for a spectacular eagle 3. From there Venturi went on to a 69 and 135, good for a four-stroke lead over Middlecoff.

Most of the gallery of twelve thousand dogged the amateur's footsteps on the third day, anticipating either a great upset or a great blowup. Venturi seemed determined to give them the blowup on the front nine. For eight holes he struggled from trees to traps, and when he missed a putt of eighteen inches on No. 9 he was out in forty strokes, and his lead was gone. Cary Middlecoff, apparently unaffected by the high-speed winds that were bothering Venturi and everyone else, went out in 35 to take over the lead by a stroke.

But on the second nine, after most of the gallery had deserted him, Venturi forged a comeback. He birdied 13, 14, and 15 in a row, playing short on both the water holes and pitching dead to the pin. He came in with 35 for a 75. Middlecoff, meanwhile, was having trouble. Cary was a chronic sufferer from hay fever. After playing nine holes he went into the clubhouse to look for his coat in which he carried a bottle of pills. But he found neither coat nor pills. A friend had worn the jacket out onto the course as protection against the blustery winds. Red-eyed and suffering, Middlecoff took a 40 on the home nine, for a 75.

Not a single player broke par, and Venturi at 210 had his four-stroke lead over Middlecoff intact. Jack Burke, playing with Venturi, also had a 75, and trailed the leader by eight strokes.

Byron Nelson, by tradition the playing partner of the leader on the final day, was expected to play with Venturi on the fourth round. But because of the close teacher-pupil relationship between the two men, the tournament committee decided it would be a mistake for Venturi to have Nelson at his side for the walk down the stretch. So Nelson was assigned elsewhere, and Venturi drew another old Master as his partner: Sam Snead.

Surrounded by a massive gallery, Venturi got no advice and little encouragement from Silent Sam. "I did talk to him a little," Snead explained later. "But after all, I was going after that first money myself." (Sam eventually finished fourth at 292.)

Ken started out playing cautiously, but well. He went out in 38 despite three three-putt greens. Middlecoff, playing just ahead of Venturi, birdied the first two holes. For a moment he stood but one stroke behind. But then Cary fell victim to some miserably erratic golf. On the 5th hole he reached the green in two and putted to within six feet of the cup. But it took him three more putts to get the ball in the hole for a double bogey 6. On the 7th hole Middlecoff dubbed an easy approach shot into a trap, the ball traveling about six feet. He took another double bogey 6. With 38 for nine holes he was still four behind Venturi. Burke played the first nine in 35 and trailed Venturi by five. Burke, playing ahead of the others, finished his round with a steady 36 for a 71. To get it he sank a long birdie putt at the 17th and another long one for a par at 18, after his approach shot landed in a trap. He was in at 289.

Middlecoff stayed in contention until the 17th. There he pitched nicely, four feet from the cup. But then, incredibly, he three-putted for another double bogey 6. Cary finished with 77-291, two strokes behind Burke.

That set the stage for Venturi. All Ken needed was a 40 on the back nine to win. He failed to get it. Venturi never really blew up on that disastrous final stretch. Instead, he kept just missing his pars. His approaches would fall just short or just over the green. The five- and six-foot putts he had been dropping all week now just missed the cup. Ken bogeyed the 10th, 11th, 12th, 14th, and 15th. Five bogeys in six holes. At the 17th he did it again. His approach rolled over the back edge of the green, and coming back he missed a ten-foot

118

Sam Snead, three-time winner of the Masters, tees
off in familiar straw hat and faultless follow through.

Jack Burke of Houston became
fifth Texan to win the Masters,
with his victory in 1956.

Beauty and peril, typical of the Augusta National,
go hand in hand on the par 3 16th hole.

try for par. That cost him the tournament. On No. 18 Venturi needed an eighteen-foot putt for a tying birdie, but again his ball just missed the cup. His card read 38-42-80, and at 290 he had lost by a stroke. Burke, the smiling Irishman, had made up nine strokes on the final round to win with a simple 71.

At the award ceremony Venturi managed a weak smile. "It was simple," he said. "I couldn't get the ball in the hole. I didn't get that green coat this year, but I'll be back."

Master champions like Wood, Guldahl, Snead, Hogan, Middlecoff, and even Burke were willing to believe Venturi would indeed be back. All six of them had finished second in the Masters before coming back to win it themselves.

1957

Caddy GEORGE FRANKLIN lifted a four iron from the bag and pleaded with his boss. "Use this one, Mistuh Ford. You gonna cost me one hundred dollars if you go in the water."

"I'm no good at playing safe," snapped burly Doug Ford. "Let's have the three wood."

Ford stood near the top of the rise on the 15th fairway. He was four under par on his final round after birdieing the 14th hole. Word had just reached him that Sam Snead, the tournament leader, was having trouble behind him. Ford needed a 245-yard carry to reach the green. He addressed the ball with almost careless brevity, swung his spoon back in an odd flat arc, and sent the ball screaming over the pond to the green. Two putts from forty feet and he was down with birdie 4. Now Doug Ford led the Masters tournament of 1957.

Ford had been born to golf in New Haven, Connecticut, where his father, Mike, was a club professional. His three uncles were pros, too, and Doug had grown up in the game on the public courses of New York City and the resorts of upstate New York—wherever work took his father. When he wasn't playing golf young Ford was usually busy in a billiard parlor, developing the same sharp stroke that he used on a golf green to become one of the most consistent putters in the game. "Doug Ford could get down in two putts from the middle of the fairway," one of his opponents once complained.

Ford developed his own approach to golf: playing the game on the dead run. Watching him play is like watching the running gunfight on a TV Western. He gallops up to the ball, pauses almost imperceptibly to aim, shoots, then gallops off again toward the next shot. Ford and his gallery can be spotted at once in any tournament. They form a flying V, as they move down the fairway. Ford is far out in front on the advance point, and the spectators, caddies, and other players tag breathlessly along in ragged lines on either side. Somehow Ford always looks like a man who is playing through the foursome he is with.

Fast play is a habit Ford formed as a boy. "After I would finish caddying or working in the golf shop there wasn't much light left to play by," he explained. "I had to play fast if I wanted to play at all. Sometimes I'd get in eighteen holes in the last ninety minutes before sundown.

"Besides," adds Ford, "when I was learning to play, Gene Sarazen's theory was popular: 'Miss 'em quick.'"

After the first round of the Masters Ford was one stroke behind the leader, Jack Burke. At 71 defending champion Burke had been the only man to break par in the record large field of 102 players.

After thirty-six holes Ford was five strokes off the pace. Sam Snead had taken the lead with a 68 for 140. With one round to go Snead still held the lead at 214 despite an erratic 74. Sam three-putted four greens and was wild off the tees. "I've been fightin' the squirrels all day," he said. "You mean to tell me I shot a 74, and I'm still leading this man's tournament? There must be some pea-picking poor golfers out there."

Snead's lead didn't last much longer. Ford started his last round three strokes behind. He had yet to break par in three days. But he quickly got down to business with birdies on the 1st and 8th holes for an outgoing 35. Snead three-putted the 8th, was trapped for a bogey on the 9th, but he also turned in 35. Ford chipped in for a deuce on the 12th hole. He added another birdie on the 14th, while Snead was taking 5's on both 10 and 11 and a 6 on No. 13, after landing in the creek. Ford's bold birdie on the 15th hole, after he outvoted his caddy, gave him the lead. Two more pars brought him to the 18th needing only a par 4 for a 67 and a probable one-stroke victory over Snead.

After a good drive on the home hole Doug hooked his seven iron into a trap at the front of the green. The ball was all but buried in the sand. Now, if ever, Ford had an excuse to change his pace, to slow down and study his lie. But he knew better. He walked into the trap, barely looked at the ball before he swung his wedge in a vicious arc. The ball rose high, dropped short of the hole, and rolled straight into the cup for a 3. Ford sent his club soaring as high as the ball. "My God," he shouted, "that's the best shot I ever made."

Ford's race-horse 66, with six birdies and twelve pars, was the best closing round ever played in the Masters. At 283 he finished three up on Snead, who came in with a 72.

Ford's brilliant finish saved the 1957 Masters from what otherwise would have been galling inconclusiveness. The tournament committee, in an attempt to streamline the un-wieldy field, which had reached 102 players, had introduced a new cut-off rule. Only the low 40 and ties qualified for the final two days of play. "We are as anxious as ever to have the older champions 'come to the party,'" explained the com-mittee. "We know that many players feel obligated to play out the full seventy-two holes even though they may not be scoring well. The new regulation automatically takes care of this particular problem. It is designed to shrink the field down to a size that could readily play two rounds, if need be,

122

in one day, and gives every contestant an afternoon pairing on the final two days."

But the new regulation brought some surprises. The older players in many cases proved hardier than the youngsters. The cut-off score turned out to be 150. Among those who failed to make the cut were Ben Hogan, putting miserably for a 151; Cary Middlecoff at 152; four other former Masters champions and a dozen of the best young players of the day. Among the qualifiers were Byron Nelson, age forty-five, Henry Picard, forty-nine, and Henry Cotton, fifty.

Middlecoff was so unhappy he packed and left town without even waiting for the annual Masters dinner that evening. Horton Smith, whose record of playing in every Masters round was broken when he missed the cut, said, "It's like being invited to dinner and then being told to leave before the dessert is served."

Some writers blamed television for the cut, figuring the tournament was being tailored to fit air-time commitments. But C.B.S. hotly denied the charge. The network was as unhappy as anyone that the Hogans and the Middlecoffs were missing from its telecast on the final two days.

Behind the sentimental sadness over the loss of so many name players was a suspicion that perhaps one of the eliminated players, Hogan in particular, might have caught up with the leaders and won the tournament. Ben was eleven strokes behind with thirty-six holes to play. He had made up that kind of ground before. And just the year before, Jack Burke had made up nine strokes on the final eighteen holes.

The grumbling grew louder on the third day when Snead held the lead despite his unimpressive 74. But Doug Ford silenced the second guessers with his closing 66. Nobody on the grounds could have beaten him that day.

1958

By 1958 it was apparent that a new generation of superbly efficient young men had taken over the game. Snead and Hogan had not won a Masters since 1954. Hogan had not won the U.S. Open since 1953. In their place the golfing boom that Hogan and Snead had helped to inspire now produced a bountiful crop of professional players, who as a group were better than any generation before them. They came by the dozens. Middlecoff, Ed Furgol, Boros, Ford, Burke, and Bolt led the "middle guard" of men over thirty. Among the young guard were Ken Venturi, Mike Souchak, Dow Finsterwald, Bill Casper, Bob Rosburg, Dick Mayer, Art Wall, Gene Littler, Fred Hawkins, Billy Maxwell, Lionel and Jay Hebert, and Arnold Palmer. Each of these men was capable of winning any given tournament any week. And each of them did.

But in the new order of things something was missing. The big galleries still followed the Hogans and the Sneads, even when they weren't winning. Each week the reporters and columnists devoted more space to retelling the exploits of

124

the old-timers than they gave to the man who won the tournament of the week. The public found it more exciting to watch the old pros on the chance they would be treated to a flash of the old-time greatness. The press complained that the new generation was an army of "faceless automatons," mechanically sound but colorless young businessmen who were practically unsortable. No sooner was each new champion built up in the public mind than he would fall back into the pack and relative obscurity. "The best golfer in the world," it was said, "is the one who won last week's tournament." Golf seemed to have fallen again into the doldrums of the thirties, when the press and the fans yearned for the personalities and matchless competition of the golden past, before the retirement of Jones. But these new doldrums, in a way, were an embarrassment of riches. So many first-class players were competing against each other every week that it became almost humanly impossible for any one, two, or even three individuals to stand out, to dominate the rest consistently. What golf needed most was a new hero, a man who would climb to the top in dramatic fashion, and more important, stay there.

Arnold Palmer was born September 10, 1929, in Latrobe, Pennsylvania. Contrary to popular legend he was not born with a golf club clutched in his hands. Arnie was at least three before his father, the Latrobe club professional, gave him his first set of cut-down clubs. He was at least five before his father taught him the most important fundamental in golf: the grip. He was at least twenty-five, a husky and muscular alumnus of the U.S. Coast Guard and Wake Forest College, when he won the U.S. Amateur championship of 1954. Arnold was a touring pro for at least six months before he won his first professional tournament, the 1955 Canadian Open.

At the 1958 Masters Arnold Palmer was one of the more promising faces in the crowd. He had won seven tournaments since his breakthrough as a rookie in the Canadian Open, and had risen on the list of money winners from thirty-second place in 1955 to fifth in 1957. The basic swing he had learned as a boy, coupled with the muscles he had developed as a man, made him tremendously long and straight off the tee. He could putt, too. If he had any weakness it was his chipping and a bold tendency to overshoot the green. He was young, strong, and had control of himself.

Scoring conditions were perfect for the opening round at Augusta, and seventeen men broke par. Ken Venturi set the pace with a 68. Venturi, now twenty-six, was established as the leading money winner on the tour. He had come back determined to capture, as a professional, the Masters championship that had escaped him as an amateur. Four players were a stroke behind Venturi at 69. Palmer had a 70, thanks to consecutive birdies at 13, 14, and 15.

On the second day Venturi again demonstrated that he is capable of the best and the worst scoring streaks in golf. The worst came on the front nine, and typical of his troubles was the 8th hole where his approach shot hit the pin. Instead of dropping dead the ball rolled thirty feet away, and Venturi took three putts to get down. He took a 7 on the hole and a 40 for the nine. But just when a repeat of his ill-famed 80 on the final round of 1956 seemed imminent, Venturi turned hot again and played the back nine in 32 strokes. He finished with birdies on the last three holes, and at 140 still held the lead. Palmer was three strokes back after a 73.

The field was again cut to the low 40 and ties, with 149 the cut-off point. Among the casualties were Jack Burke, the 1956 winner, and Dick Mayer, 1957 U.S. Open champion.

Venturi slipped to a 74 on the third day and skidded down the list to 214. The field rushed in to replace him, and by evening the co-leaders were old Sam Snead and young Arnold Palmer. Each had shot 68 to tie at 211 with one round to go.

A dozen players were bunched between 211 and 215, as the final day began. All-night rains left the course soggy and slow. The rains cleared by morning, but the tournament committee decided conditions were bad enough to invoke a U.S.G.A. "wet weather" rule, which permitted the players to lift, clean, and drop without penalty any ball which became

126

imbedded in its own pit mark "through the green." The latter term included all parts of the course except hazards.

Palmer teed off first among the contenders, and began the nerve-racking job of leading the Masters down the stretch. Snead took a 6 on the first hole and never got back on his game. But the others kept coming. Venturi, playing with Palmer, went out in 35, one less than Arnold. When Palmer bogeyed No. 10 Venturi had cut his deficit to one stroke, as the two men headed into Amen Corner. In their own oblique way the 12th and 13th holes again decided the tournament.

Both Venturi and Palmer hit their tee shots over the 12th green and onto the bank behind. Venturi's ball kicked back down onto the edge of the green and left him with a routine 3, which he proceeded to make. Palmer's ball imbedded itself in the bank about a foot from the edge of a trap. Palmer hit the half-buried ball with his wedge. It rolled about eighteen inches into some casual water. Palmer lifted and dropped it without penalty and finally chipped close to the pin on his third shot. He missed the putt and took a 5. This put him a stroke behind Venturi.

But the 12th hole wasn't over for Palmer. He played out his original ball without any relief, then remembering the "wet weather" rule he returned to the spot where his ball had been buried and dropped a provisional ball. This move had been approved by the rules committee official with the understanding that the general chairman of the rules committee would be asked for a final decision as to which of the two scores made—the one with the original ball or the provisional one—would be counted. Palmer chipped this provisional ball dead to the pin, and this time he holed the putt. Now the question was: Did Palmer score a 3 or a 5?

The official answer would take awhile, and in the meantime Palmer and Venturi teed off on No. 13. Venturi's drive was short. He decided to play his second shot short of the creek and take his chances on getting down in two from there. Palmer, apparently unrattled by his troubles on the 12th, hit a powerful drive that carried 250 yards before it landed in soft turf. From there Arnold decided to go for the green. He hit a three wood shot that rose in a right-to-left trajectory and landed comfortably hole high, eighteen feet to the left of the cup. At this point Palmer received word—not official yet, but on good authority—that his provisional 3 on No. 12 would be allowed to stand. He responded by holing out his eighteen-footer for an eagle 3 on No. 13. Venturi, meanwhile, had pitched on and sunk his putt for a gallant birdie 4. But instead of being a stroke ahead as he appeared to be on the 13th tee, Venturi was now two behind with five holes to play.

On the 14th Venturi three-putted and fell another stroke back. On the 15th hole Palmer was notified that his 3 was official. Venturi three-putted again. On 16 he did the same. Ken finished with a birdie on the 18th for a 72 and a 286 total. Palmer also wobbled a little in the stretch with bogeys on 16 and 18, and these indiscretions earned him another hour of nightmarish tension. Palmer finished with 73-284.

A twosome made up of Doug Ford, the defending champion, and Fred Hawkins was sprinting down the stretch with a chance to catch the leader. At the 18th green each man needed a birdie putt to tie. But as a national C.B.S. television audience watched, Hawkins missed from sixteen feet and Ford missed from twelve. The Masters and golf had a new champion in Arnold Palmer, a power hitter who knew the rules and who could contain himself under pressure.

1959

ARNOLD PALMER was back at the 12th hole. For the second year in a row Arnie was leading the Masters down the stretch, this time as defending champion. From his 1958 Masters victory he had gone on to lead the circuit with $42,000 in winnings. In this 1959 Masters he had taken over the lead after thirty-six holes, and he still held it on this final day. His major challenge had come from Stan Leonard, the Canadian champion. Leonard led the first round and came back to tie Palmer for the lead after three rounds. But now Leonard was floundering badly on the last round. Palmer had still another challenge to overcome: the jinx that no man ever wins the Masters two years in a row. Over thirty thousand people, perhaps more than had ever squeezed onto a golf course before, had come to see if Arnold could break the jinx.

Palmer, durable and steady, was doing fine. With seven holes to go he was even with par. Now he took aim on the 12th green, 155 yards away. Now he swung his iron. And now he plunked the ball into the middle of Rae's Creek. Palmer

129

hit again. This time he cleared the water but missed the green. He finished the hole with a 6—triple bogey. Suddenly Palmer needed to make up ground. With powerful strokes he earned his bird on No. 13 and again on No. 15. At 14 and 16 he got par. But on the 17th green he stood two feet away from his par, tapped the putt, and missed. Still fighting he sent his approach on the 18th four feet from the cup. A birdie might still give him the championship. But once more his putt rolled over a corner of the hole and stayed out. Palmer was finished with a 74 and 286.

Playing behind Palmer was slender, little Art Wall, Jr., a fellow Pennsylvanian and one of the quietest men in golf. At thirty-five Art had been around for quite awhile. Nobody considered him much of a threat for the Masters, even though he was enjoying his best year. He had the best record of anybody on the winter circuit and was fresh from a victory in the Azalea Open. Wall did little to attract attention as he started with a 73 and followed that with a 74. At 147 he survived the cut-off by a bare two strokes. A 71 in the third round left him in a tie for thirteenth place at 218. "The best thing you can say about my game," he said, "is that I'm not making as many mistakes as I was. Oh, and I've been putting pretty well all year." Wall was six strokes behind the leaders, and he had never broken 70 in a Masters round.

At about the time Palmer was missing his two-footer on the 17th Art Wall struck. He hit a wood to the edge of the 13th green. A chip shot from eighty feet left him short, but he dropped the fifteen-foot putt for a birdie. At the 14th, twenty feet from the hole at the back edge of the green, Wall rolled in his putt for another birdie. On the 15th the television cameras picked him up, and millions of viewers gasped in their living rooms as his eagle putt from twenty-five feet just skirted the edge of the cup. The next putt went down for a birdie. On No. 16 he needed two putts to get in from ten feet. But on the 17th hole Wall's partner, Julius Boros, said to him, "You can scare somebody with another birdie." Wall obliged with a fifteen-foot putt for his 3.

130

Now a par would beat Palmer. Wall sent his tee shot on the final hole three hundred yards to the left-hand side of the fairway. "It was my best drive of the tournament," he said. The pin was set in the front right section of the green, and Wall went for it with a nine iron. The ball landed twelve feet below the cup, just where he wanted it. He rolled in the putt for another bird. It gave him a 66-284.

By shooting birdies on five of the last six holes of the tournament Wall had beaten Palmer by two strokes. As it turned out he needed the extra stroke. Cary Middlecoff, bolstered by an eagle at the 15th, needed just one birdie on the last three holes to tie Wall. But Cary missed putts of twenty, fourteen, and twenty-five feet on the last three greens, and finished one stroke behind.

Quiet Art Wall had found a dramatic way to join the Masters.

1960

ARNOLD PALMER marched on Augusta like Sherman on Atlanta. In February at Palm Springs he won the Desert Classic. At Tucson he tied for fifth place. At San Antonio, a week later, he won the Texas Open. Moving eastward he won the Baton Rouge Open in the first week of March. Seven days later he won at Pensacola, his third straight. At St. Petersburg he finished fifth and tied for fifth again in the DeSoto Open at Bradenton. Then, with four fresh titles and $26,000 already in hand, Palmer turned north to Augusta.

Despite his arrival a week early Arnold managed only four practice rounds on the National course. Cold, rainy weather kept the course closed much of the time, and put Palmer in bed temporarily with a case of flu. The rain clouds had their sunny side for Palmer. The course became soggy and slow, and played even longer than its listed 6,980 yards. This was an advantage for the very long hitters: Sam Snead, Mike Souchak, and Arnold Palmer.

Power itself cannot win the Masters. As Bob Jones whimsically put it, "A long driver has a definite advantage over a short driver, if he hits his long drive in the right direction." But by the eve of the competition it was no secret that it would be Arnold Palmer against the field in this twenty-fourth renewal of the Masters.

The "field" was no mean collection. For the first time it did not include a defending champion. Art Wall, the 1959 winner, was recovering from a kidney infection and a bad knee. He had to stand by and watch. But every other Masters champion except Ralph Guldahl was there. Ten foreign players representing nine countries, led by Gary Player of South Africa and Stan Leonard of Canada, were on hand. Seventeen amateurs, including Jack Nicklaus, the U.S. champion, Deane Beman, the British champion, Billy Joe Patton, Charles Coe, and Ward Wettlaufer were among the eighty-eight entrants. No amateur and no foreign player had ever finished first.

Ben Hogan was contending for his third championship. Snead and Jimmy Demaret were aiming for their fourth. Others, like Billy Casper and Bob Rosburg, Ken Venturi, Dow Finsterwald, Ed Furgol, Julius Boros, the brothers Hebert, and Mike Souchak were determined to join the exclusive fraternity that had so far been denied to them.

The traditional pretournament driving contest was replaced by a par-3 competition. It was held on a tiny but lovely three-and-a-half-acre layout built around a pond just behind "Mamie's cabin," the cottage the Eisenhowers had made famous as their vacation retreat. Snead won this friendly joust by playing the nine holes in twenty-three strokes, four under par. Palmer finished in a tie for fifth at 25. Said he, "I don't know what will happen when the big one begins, but I'm hitting the ball fairly good and if I can just keep everything organized I'll be all right." Then he retreated to his motel, watched *Wagon Train* on TV for an hour, and went to bed.

The next afternoon Arnold Palmer shot a 67, five under par, to take over the first round lead in the 1960 Masters. Two venerable citizens, Fred McLeod and Jock Hutchinson, filled their annual role as the opening twosome a few minutes

133

before 10 A.M. By the time Palmer teed off at noon a record Thursday crowd of upward of fifteen thousand was on the grounds. Arnold treated them to a birdie on the first hole, sticking his six iron approach a few feet from the pin. At No. 2 he birdied again, after reaching the par five green in two. At the 8th he exploded out of a trap into the cup for an eagle 3. At 13 and 15 he birdied again. The 67 was a tribute to the power of Palmer's iron wrists and muscular shoulders. On the four par-5 holes he scored three birdies and an eagle.

As Palmer finished his round Ken Venturi was finishing the front line. Putting masterfully on the slower-than-usual greens, Venturi was off to the fastest start in tournament history, with a blistering 31 on the opening nine. He parred the 10th, three-putted the 11th for a bogey, then struck a tee shot on No. 12 that hit the green and bounced over.

Earlier on this same 12th hole Palmer had gone beyond the green with his tee shot and stopped in a bad lie at the top of the bunker. Palmer asked for and got a free drop under the "wet weather" rule he remembered so well from 1958. He parred the hole.

Venturi's shot landed in a pockmark left from a previous ball. Ken could scarcely see his ball. But the official at the hole, P.G.A. secretary Ed Carter, ruled that since the ball had hit the green first and had not become imbedded on its own the rule did not apply and Venturi would have to play out. Ken gamely hacked out of the hole, chipped on with his next shot, and got down in two putts for a 5. That reversal undid Venturi. From very hot he turned to freezing cold. He three-putted 14 and 15 and lost another stroke at 18, where his second shot landed next to a TV tower. Venturi handed in a card of 31-42-73. Once more he must have felt like a man riding a yo-yo.

Two strokes behind Palmer at 69 were four tough pros: Dow Finsterwald, Fred Hawkins, Jay Hebert, and Claude Harmon. Harmon, now forty-four, chuckled over finishing ahead of any of his "chickens" from Winged Foot.

On the second day Arnold Palmer's feet hurt. The new

134

shoes he had broken in two days before were giving him trouble, adding to the burden of pressure on him. At the 5th hole Arnold tore off a piece of scorecard and stuffed it in his right shoe to protect the blister that was developing. Three bogeys on the first eight holes staggered him, but he trudged through the final ten holes in two under par for a 73. At 140 he still led the field by a stroke.

Dow Finsterwald gained three strokes on Palmer with a 70, and would have taken over the lead but for a belated penalty. The day before, after he had finished playing the 5th hole, Finsterwald had stopped to take a practice putt. The rule against this was printed on his scorecard and Dow discovered it the next day and reported his misdemeanor to the rules committee. Under the rules he could have been disqualified for turning in a wrong score. Instead, he was penalized two strokes. That put him at 141, a stroke behind Palmer. Also at 141 were Wally Burkemo, Harmon, and Ben Hogan. Hogan counted himself in with the best round of the day, a 68. Ken Venturi, recovering quickly from his opening day fiasco, came back with a 69 and was two strokes behind at 142.

Under a modified cut-off rule the low 40 and ties plus any player within ten strokes of the leader qualified for the final thirty-six holes. Forty-five survived. Those who didn't included Byron Nelson, who had never been cut before, Horton Smith, Cary Middlecoff, and five other former champions. But by now the cut-off was generally accepted as a necessary part of the tournament.

It was like old times in the clubhouse, as reporters packed around Ben Hogan. "Are you fellows waiting for me, or are you holding a meeting?", joked Hogan. "I felt the same as I always do," he told them, "my nerves were driving me crazy on the greens. But today some of those putts went in."

Then it was Venturi's turn. "After that forty-two yesterday a thirty-five on the back nine looked pretty good to me today. I'm relaxed again now."

Said Palmer, "I'm lucky to still be in front."

And Finsterwald, who had sweated out a long meeting

135

of the rules committee, added, *"I'm* lucky just to be still in the tournament."

Attendance had swelled to over twenty thousand on Friday, and for Saturday's third round it reached thirty thousand. Palmer walked through blustery winds with an angry blister on his heel. From tee to green he was his usual, overpowering self. Only his putter gave away any sign that Arnold was working under pressure. He three-putted twice and once he missed a four-footer after a good chip shot. In all he used thirty-three putts to get an even par 72. "I putted like Joe Schmoe," said Arnie. His total was 212.

The field closed in but couldn't quite catch him. Five men clustered a step behind Palmer, at 213, for the tightrope walk down the stretch. They were Hogan, Venturi, Finsterwald, and two new contenders, Boros and Casper. Nine more players stood at par or better and were still within reach.

Upward of thirty-five thousand people converged on the Augusta National to see the final round for themselves. The single question in their minds: Could the calm, commanding young athlete from Latrobe, Pennsylvania, hold off the field for a fourth straight day?

The going was rough from the start. Hogan, Boros, and Casper quickly made it obvious that they weren't going to make a run for it. Casper slipped to an eventual 74, Boros to 75, and Hogan to 76. That left three for the money.

Venturi and Finsterwald teed off together an hour ahead of Palmer. While Finsterwald struggled for pars Venturi birdied three of the first six holes and took the lead. Neither man went over par on the front nine. But Finsterwald birdied the 8th and 9th to pull within a stroke of Venturi. Ken was out in 33, Dow in 34. The two men played down the treacherous back nine head-to-head. When Venturi bogeyed the 11th Finsterwald pulled even. But Dow lost that stroke with a bogey on No. 12. A birdie at 14 brought Finsterwald even again and he stayed there until the 18th green. On that final hole Finsterwald's two iron approach caught a trap to the right. He chipped out eight feet past the cup, then missed his putt for a bogey 5 and 284. Venturi took his par for a 70-283. Once more Ken Venturi was within tasting distance of the Masters title. His bid was in.

Arnold Palmer opened his final round with a birdie. His putter was on. But at the 3rd he three-putted. His putter was off.

At the 4th he bogeyed again and lost the lead to Venturi. But a birdie at No. 5 got it back, and he finished the first nine in 36, even par. From Nos. 10 through 14 Palmer strung pars together. By now the all-too-handy scoreboards showed him that Venturi was in with a 70 and a total five under par. Palmer sorely needed birdies, one to tie and two to win.

His drive on the 15th left him with two trees and the pond between him and the flag. He elected to go for it, around the trees. His shot carried the water and stopped pin high, but far to the right in the middle of the giant gallery and close to the foot of a scoreboard. Palmer took ten minutes to clear a channel to the green, moving people and carefully picking up the paper debris they left behind. Finally he chipped up and on, but the ball stopped fifteen feet short of the cup. Palmer flipped his club to his caddy, and the caddy, a lad named Ironman, glowered back at him.

"That look on Ironman's face is the same one my pap used to give me," thought Palmer. "The last time he saw me throw a club he said to me, 'If you ever do that again, I'll take your clubs away and you'll never play golf again.' I'd better calm down."

Palmer putted twice; par 5, but no birdie.

For the 16th hole Arnold chose a four iron. "This might not be enough club," he thought, but his shot dropped onto the front of the green. He putted and the ball ran hard for the hole, hit the pin, and bounced off. Par 3, but no birdie. Palmer was running out of holes. On No. 17 he drove long to the right side of the fairway. It was on this hole he had lost the tournament a year before. Consistently here he had gone over on his approach. "Keep the ball short of the cup," Palmer told himself. "Give it plenty of stuff and make it stop."

137

The pitch rose and stopped all right, some thirty-five feet short of the hole. Palmer waited until his partner, Casper, had putted out. Then he lined up his putt and sent it on the long, rolling trip to the cup. It fell in, and Palmer leaped spread-eagled off the ground, with a mighty war whoop that was lost in the shout of the crowd. Birdie 3, all even.

Palmer's drive home carried almost three hundred yards down the center of the 18th fairway. A six iron to the green flew six feet from the hole. Now most of the huge gallery tried to force in around the green. Ralph Hutchinson, the field announcer, asked for quiet. In the clubhouse Venturi fidgeted before a television set.

A year before Palmer had missed a four-footer on the seventy-second hole from the same position. That putt had gone to the left. "This time give it room to break," he told himself, as he lined up his putt to the right. Break it did, squarely into the cup—birdie 3.

The two closing birdies made Palmer Master again. The crowd swept in on him as he threaded his way to the clubhouse, weary and grinning and hugging his wife. His reward for winning the 1960 Masters was $17,500 out of a total pot of $87,050. Both figures were records. Each of the first ten finishers received more than the $1,500 Horton Smith had taken home in 1934. Last place in the field was worth $350, in this richest of all tournaments.

Two months later Palmer would produce another stirring finish to win the U.S. Open. By October he would be elected golfer of the year. But this was the moment that established him as something more than a winning golfer. He became a memorable part of the Masters tradition.

Ken Venturi was among the first to congratulate Palmer. "I'll be back," promised Ken.

"So will I," warned Arnold.

In a quiet corner of the locker room another young golfer made the same promise to himself. "I'll be back."

"I hope you'll all be back," said Bob Jones. "And I hope you all had a good time."

APPENDIX

The first ten finishers and ties of the Masters,

1934-1960

1934

Horton Smith	70	72	70	72	284
Craig Wood	71	74	69	71	285
Billy Burke	72	71	70	73	286
Paul Runyan	74	71	70	71	286
Ed Dudley	74	69	71	74	288
Willie Macfarlane	74	73	70	74	291
Harold McSpaden	77	74	72	69	292
Al Espinosa	75	70	75	72	292
Jimmy Hines	70	74	74	74	292
Macdonald Smith	74	70	74	74	292

1935

Gene Sarazen	68	71	73	70	282
Play off					144
Craig Wood	69	72	68	73	282
Play off					149
Olin Dutra	70	70	70	74	284
Henry Picard	67	68	76	75	286
Denny Shute	73	71	70	73	287
Lawson Little, Jr.	74	72	70	72	288
Paul Runyan	70	72	75	72	289
Vic Ghezzi	73	71	73	73	290
Jimmy Hines	70	70	77	74	291
Byron Nelson, Jr.	71	74	72	74	291
Bobby Cruickshank	76	70	73	72	291
Joe Turnesa	73	71	74	73	291

1936

Horton Smith	74	71	68	72	285
Harry Cooper	70	69	71	76	286
Gene Sarazen	78	67	72	70	287
Bobby Cruickshank	75	69	74	72	290
Paul Runyan	76	69	70	75	290
Ray Mangrum	76	73	68	76	293
Ed Dudley	75	75	70	73	293
Ky Laffoon	75	70	75	73	293
John Dawson	77	70	70	77	294
Henry Picard	75	72	74	73	294

1937

Byron Nelson	66	72	75	70	283
Ralph Guldahl	69	72	68	76	285
Ed Dudley	70	71	71	74	286
Harry Cooper	73	69	71	74	287
Ky Laffoon	73	70	74	73	290
Jimmy Thomson	71	73	74	73	291
Al Watrous	74	72	71	75	292
Tommy Armour	73	75	73	72	293
Vic Ghezzi	72	72	72	77	293
Jimmy Hines	77	72	68	77	294
Leonard Dodson	71	75	71	77	294

1938

Henry Picard	71	72	72	70	285
Ralph Guldahl	73	70	73	71	287
Harry Cooper	68	77	71	71	287
Paul Runyan	71	73	74	70	288
Byron Nelson	73	74	70	73	290
Ed Dudley	70	69	77	75	291
Felix Serafin	72	71	78	70	291
Dick Metz	70	77	74	71	292
Jimmy Thomson	74	70	76	72	292
Jimmy Hines	75	71	75	72	293
Vic Ghezzi	75	74	70	74	293
Lawson Little, Jr.	72	75	74	72	293

1939

Ralph Guldahl	72	68	70	69	279
Sam Snead	70	70	72	68	280
Billy Burke	69	72	71	70	282
Lawson Little, Jr.	72	72	68	70	282
Gene Sarazen	73	66	72	72	283
Craig Wood	72	73	71	68	284
Byron Nelson	71	69	72	75	287
Henry Picard	71	71	76	71	289
Ben Hogan	75	71	72	72	290
Toney Penna	72	75	72	72	291
Ed Dudley	75	75	69	72	291

1940

Jimmy Demaret	67	72	70	71	280
Lloyd Mangrum	64	75	71	74	284
Byron Nelson	69	72	74	70	285
Ed Dudley	73	72	71	71	287
Harry Cooper	69	75	73	70	287
Willie Goggin	71	72	73	71	287
Henry Picard	71	71	71	75	288
Craig Wood	70	75	67	76	288
Sam Snead	71	72	69	76	288
Toney Penna	73	73	72	72	290
Ben Hogan	73	74	69	74	290

1941

Craig Wood	66	71	71	72	280
Byron Nelson	71	69	73	70	283
Sam Byrd	73	70	68	74	285
Ben Hogan	71	72	75	68	286
Ed Dudley	73	72	75	68	288
Sam Snead	73	75	72	69	289
Vic Ghezzi	77	71	71	70	289
Lawson Little, Jr.	71	70	74	75	290
Lloyd Mangrum	71	72	72	76	291
Harold McSpaden	75	74	72	70	291
Willie Goggin	71	72	72	76	291

1942

Byron Nelson	68	67	72	73	280
Play off					69
Ben Hogan	73	70	67	70	280
Play off					70
Paul Runyan	67	73	72	71	283
Sam Byrd	68	68	75	74	285
Horton Smith	67	73	74	73	287
Jimmy Demaret	70	70	75	75	290
E. J. Harrison	74	70	71	77	292
Lawson Little, Jr.	71	74	72	75	292
Sam Snead	78	69	72	73	292
Gene Kunes	74	74	74	71	293
Chick Harbert	73	73	72	75	293

1946

Herman Keiser	69	68	71	74	282
Ben Hogan	74	70	69	70	283
Bob Hamilton	75	69	71	72	287
Ky Laffoon	74	73	70	72	289
Jimmy Demaret	75	70	71	73	289
Jim Ferrier	74	72	68	75	289
Sam Snead	74	75	70	71	290
Clayton Heafner	74	69	71	76	290
Byron Nelson	72	73	71	74	290
Chick Harbert	69	75	76	70	290

1947

Jimmy Demaret	69	71	70	71	281
Byron Nelson	69	72	72	70	283
Frank Stranahan	73	72	70	68	283
Ben Hogan	75	68	71	70	284
Harold McSpaden	74	69	70	71	284
Henry Picard	73	70	72	71	286
Jim Ferrier	70	71	73	72	286
Ed Oliver, Jr.	70	72	74	71	287
Chandler Harper	77	72	68	70	287
Lloyd Mangrum	76	73	68	70	287
Toney Penna	71	70	75	71	287
Dick Metz	72	72	72	71	287

1948

Claude Harmon	70	70	69	70	279
Cary Middlecoff	74	71	69	70	284
Chick Harbert	71	70	70	76	287
Jim Ferrier	71	71	75	71	288
Lloyd Mangrum	69	73	75	71	288
Ed Furgol	70	72	73	74	289
Ben Hogan	70	71	77	71	289
Byron Nelson	71	73	72	74	290
Harry Todd	72	67	80	71	290
Herman Keiser	70	72	76	73	291
Bobby Locke	71	71	74	75	291
Dick Metz	71	72	75	73	291

1949

Sam Snead	73	75	67	67	282
Johnny Bulla	74	73	69	69	285
Lloyd Mangrum	69	74	72	70	285
Johnny Palmer	73	71	70	72	286
Jim Turnesa	73	72	71	70	286
Lew Worsham, Jr.	76	75	70	68	289
Joe Kirkwood, Jr.	73	72	70	75	290
Jimmy Demaret	76	72	73	71	292
Clayton Heafner	71	74	72	75	292
Byron Nelson	75	70	74	73	292

1950

Jimmy Demaret	70	72	72	69	283
Jim Ferrier	70	67	73	75	285
Sam Snead	71	74	70	72	287
Ben Hogan	73	68	71	76	288
Byron Nelson	75	70	69	74	288
Lloyd Mangrum	76	74	73	68	291
Clayton Heafner	74	77	69	72	292
Cary Middlecoff	75	76	68	73	292
Lawson Little, Jr.	70	73	75	75	293
Fred Haas, Jr.	74	76	73	71	294
Gene Sarazen	80	70	72	72	294

1951

Ben Hogan	70	72	70	68	280
Skee Riegel	73	68	70	71	282
Lloyd Mangrum	69	74	70	73	286
Lew Worsham, Jr.	71	71	72	72	286
Dave Douglas	74	69	72	73	288
Lawson Little, Jr.	72	73	72	72	289
Jim Ferrier	74	70	74	72	290
Johnny Bulla	71	72	73	75	291
Byron Nelson	71	73	73	74	291
Sam Snead	69	74	68	80	291

1952

Sam Snead	70	67	77	72	286
Jack Burke, Jr.	76	67	78	69	290
Al Besselink	70	76	71	74	291
Tommy Bolt	71	71	75	74	291
Jim Ferrier	72	70	77	72	291
Lloyd Mangrum	71	74	75	72	292
Julius Boros	73	73	76	71	293
Fred Hawkins	71	73	78	71	293
Ben Hogan	70	70	74	79	293
Lew Worsham, Jr.	71	75	73	74	293

1953

Ben Hogan	70	69	66	69	274
Ed Oliver, Jr.	69	73	67	70	279
Lloyd Mangrum	74	68	71	69	282
Bob Hamilton	71	69	70	73	283
Tommy Bolt	71	75	68	71	285
Chick Harbert	68	73	70	74	285
Ted Kroll	71	70	73	72	286
Jack Burke, Jr.	78	69	69	71	287
Al Besselink	69	75	70	74	288
Julius Boros	73	71	75	70	289
Chandler Harper	74	72	69	74	289
Fred Hawkins	75	70	74	70	289

1954

Sam Snead	74	73	70	72	289
Play off					70
Ben Hogan	72	73	69	75	289
Play off					71
(Billy Joe) Patton	70	74	75	71	290
E. J. Harrison	70	79	74	68	291
Lloyd Mangrum	71	75	76	69	291
Jerry Barber	74	76	71	71	292
Jack Burke, Jr.	71	77	73	71	292
Bob Rosburg	73	73	76	70	292
Al Besselink	74	74	74	72	294
Cary Middlecoff	73	76	70	75	294

1955

Cary Middlecoff	72	65	72	70	279
Ben Hogan	73	68	72	73	286
Sam Snead	72	71	74	70	287
Bob Rosburg	72	72	72	73	289
Mike Souchak	71	74	72	72	289
Julius Boros	71	75	72	71	289
Lloyd Mangrum	74	73	72	72	291
Harvie Ward	77	69	75	71	292
Stan Leonard	77	73	68	74	292
Dick Mayer	78	72	72	71	293
Byron Nelson	72	75	74	72	293
Arnold Palmer	76	76	72	69	293

1956

Jack Burke, Jr.	72	71	75	71	289
Ken Venturi	66	69	75	80	290
Cary Middlecoff	67	72	75	77	291
Lloyd Mangrum	72	74	72	74	292
Sam Snead	73	76	72	71	292
Jerry Barber	71	72	76	75	294
Doug Ford	70	72	75	77	294
Shelley Mayfield	68	74	80	74	296
Tommy Bolt	68	74	78	76	296
Ben Hogan	69	78	74	75	296

1957

Doug Ford	72	73	72	66	283
Sam Snead	72	68	74	72	286
Jimmy Demaret	72	70	75	70	287
Harvie Ward	73	71	71	73	288
Peter Thomson	72	73	73	71	289
Ed Furgol	73	71	72	74	290
Jack Burke, Jr.	71	72	74	74	291
Dow Finsterwald	74	74	73	70	291
Arnold Palmer	73	73	69	76	291
Jay Hebert	74	72	76	70	292

1958

Arnold Palmer	70	73	68	73	284
Doug Ford	74	71	70	70	285
Fred Hawkins	71	75	68	71	285
Stan Leonard	72	70	73	71	286
Ken Venturi	68	72	74	72	286
Cary Middlecoff	70	73	69	75	287
Art Wall, Jr.	71	72	70	74	287
Billy Joe Patton	72	69	73	74	288
Claude Harmon	71	76	72	70	289
Jay Hebert	72	73	73	71	289
Billy Maxwell	71	70	72	76	289
Al Mengert	73	71	69	76	289

1959

Art Wall, Jr.	73	74	71	66	284
Cary Middlecoff	74	71	68	72	285
Arnold Palmer	71	70	71	74	286
Dick Mayer	73	75	71	68	287
Stan Leonard	69	74	69	75	287
Charles R. Coe	74	74	67	73	288
Fred Hawkins	77	71	68	73	289
Julius Boros	75	69	74	72	290
Jay Hebert	72	73	72	73	290
Gene Littler	72	75	72	71	290
Billy Maxwell	73	71	72	74	290
Billy Joe Patton	75	70	71	74	290
Gary Player	73	75	71	71	290

1960

Arnold Palmer	67	73	72	70	282
Ken Venturi	73	69	71	70	283
Dow Finsterwald	71	70	72	71	284
Bill Casper	71	71	71	74	287
Julius Boros	72	71	70	75	288
Gary Player	72	71	72	74	289
Wally Burkemo	72	69	75	73	289
Ben Hogan	73	68	72	76	289
Lionel Hebert	74	70	73	73	290
Stan Leonard	72	72	72	74	290

144

SELECTED BIBLIOGRAPHY

Magazines

Life
P.G.A. Professional Golfer
Sports Illustrated
Time
Town and Country

Newspapers

Augusta *Chronicle*
Augusta *Herald*
New York *Herald Tribune*
New York *World-Telegram*
New York *Times*

Book

Herbert Warren Wind:
   The Story of American Golf

INDEX

De Soto Open, 132
Desert Classic, 132
Dey, Joe, 106
Dodson, Leonard, 141
Douglas, Dave, 143
Dudley, Ed, 8, 19-22, 26, 36-8, 41-2, 50, 59, 64, 141-2
Dunphy, Chris, 82
Dutra, Mortie, 22
Dutra, Olin, 26-7, 141

East Lake Club, 4, 20
Eisenhower, Dwight D., 102, 133
Espinosa, Al, 22, 32, 141

Fazio, George, 95-6
Ferrier, James (Jim), 80, 92-4, 142-3
Finsterwald, Dow, 98, 124, 133-6, 144
Firestone Club, 72-3
Ford, Douglas (Doug), 120-4, 128, 144
Ford, Michael (Mike), 120
Franklin, George, 120
French, Emmett, 19
Furgol, Ed, 83, 124, 133, 142, 144

Ghezzi, Vic, 74, 141-2
Glen Garden (golf club), 37, 62-3
Goggin, Willie, 26, 142
Golden, Jimmy, 19
Golden, John, 16
Goodman, Johnny, 45
Grand Slam, 3, 101
Greater Greensboro Open, 72
Greenbrier (golf club), 87
Greiner, Otto, 83
Guldahl, Ralph, 35-9, 42, 44-8, 50, 59, 68-70, 74, 85, 87, 95, 102, 119, 133, 141

Haas, Fred, Jr., 74, 143
Hagen, Walter ("Haig"), 19-22, 24, 27, 29, 40-1, 45, 51, 74, 78, 89
Hamilton, Bob, 71, 142-3

Harbert, Chick, 70, 73-4, 83-4, 102, 142-3
Harmon, Claude, 82-5, 102, 111, 134-5, 142, 144
Harper, Chandler, 70-1, 73, 142-3
Harrison, E. J. ("Dutch"), 105, 142-3
Hawkins, Fred, 124, 128, 134, 143-4
Heafner, Clayton, 142-3
Hebert, Jay, 124, 133-4, 144
Hebert, Lionel, 124, 133, 144
Hickory Hills Country Club, 72
Hines, Jimmy, 19, 22, 64, 141
Hogan, William Benjamin (Ben), 18, 39, 41, 48, 50, 55, 58-9, 63-72, 74-7, 80, 83-4, 86-7, 90, 92-114, 116, 119, 123-4, 133, 135-6, 141-4
"Hogan's Alley," 92
Hutchinson, Jock, 133
Hutchinson, Ralph, 138

Iowa State Open, 72

Jones, Colonel Robert P., 20
Jones, Robert Tyre, Jr. (Bobby), 3-8, 12-22, 24-33, 38-9, 45, 47, 50-1, 53-4, 64, 66, 70, 74, 80, 83, 90-1, 97, 101-2, 104, 111-2, 125, 132, 138

Keeler, O. B., 4, 15, 71
Keiser, Herman, 71-7, 80, 88-9, 93, 96, 102, 142
Kinder, Johnny, 16
Kirkwood, Joe, 25
Kirkwood, Joe, Jr., 143
Korean War, 98
Kroll, Ted, 143
Kunes, Gene, 142

Laffoon, Ky, 141-2
Leonard, Stanley (Stan), 129, 133, 144
Little, Lawson, Jr., 32-4, 47-8, 50, 71, 141-3
Littler, Gene, 124, 144

148